The Theatre and Drama of Greece and Rome

Chandler Publications in History of Theatre
Dunbar H. Ogden *and* Alois M. Nagler, *Editors*

THE THEATRE AND DRAMA OF GREECE AND ROME

JAMES H. BUTLER
University of Southern California

CHANDLER PUBLISHING COMPANY
An Intext Publisher
SAN FRANCISCO • SCRANTON • LONDON • TORONTO

Library of Congress Cataloging in Publication Data

Butler, James H
  The theatre and drama of Greece and Rome.
    xv, 164 p. ill. 23 cm ③
  (Chandler publications in history of theatre)
  Bibliography: p. 145–146.
    1. Theater—Greece. 2. Theater—Rome.
3. Classical drama—History and criticism. I. Title.
PA3201.B8   792'.0938   74–164495
ISBN 0–8102–0439–8

To Willena

CONTENTS

ILLUSTRATIONS   xi

PREFACE   xv

1. GREEK DRAMA: ORIGIN AND DEVELOPMENT   1

Dithyrambs   4
Tragedies   5
Aeschylus / Sophocles / Euripides / Tragedies after Euripides /
   Structure of a Tragedy
Satyr Plays   13
Old Comedy   16
Middle Comedy   23
New Comedy   24

2. GREEK THEATRES   27

Cretan "Theatral Areas"   28
The Earliest Athenian Theatre   29
Classical Theatres   29
Theatre of Dionysus / Theatre of Epidauros
Hellenistic Theatres   39
Theatre of Priene / Other Important Theatres / Possible Origins of the
   Skene / Hellenistic Theatres in Retrospect
Current Use of Ancient Theatres   48

3. THEATRICAL PRODUCTION IN GREECE   50

Theatre Festivals   50
Rural Dionysia / Lenaea / City Dionysia
Tragedies, Comedies, and Satyr Plays in Production   55
Producers / Directors and Actors / The Chorus / Masks /
    Costumes / Production and Acting Styles
Dithyrambs and Doric Mimes in Production   66
Stage Scenery and Machinery   67
Audiences   69

4. ROMAN THEATRE: DRAMA AND OTHER FORMS   72

Etruscan Dances and Fescennine Verses   72
Saturae   73
Atellan Farces   73
Mimes   75
Pantomimes   76
Phlyakes   77
Tragic Recitations   78
Pyrrhic Dances   79
Tragedies and Comedies   79
Plautus / Terence

5. ROMAN THEATRES   87

Phlyake Stages   88
Hellenistic Theatres of Sicily and Pompeii   90
Temporary Wooden Theatres   90
Odea   92
Permanent Stone Theatres   94
Theatre of Pompey / Theatre of Balbus / Theatre of Marcellus
Greco-Roman Theatres   98
Theatres according to Vitruvius   101
Stone Theatres of the Empire   103
Roman Theatres in Retrospect   107

6. THEATRICAL PRODUCTION IN ROME   109

Ludi   109
Ludi Scaenici / Finances for Ludi
Tragedies and Comedies in Production   111

Producers / Managers and Actors / Production and Acting Styles /
Masks / Costumes
Atellan Farces, Mimes, and Pantomimes in Production   118
Actors, Companies, and Acting Styles / Masks and Costumes
Stage Scenery and Machinery   123
Audiences: Republic and Empire   125

7. GAMES AND SPECTACLES IN ROME   127

Circuses   128
Amphitheatres   133
The Colosseum
Gladiatorial Games   137
Venationes   139
Naumachiae   141
Games and Spectacles in Retrospect   143

SUGGESTED READINGS AND FILMSTRIPS   145
Theatre and Drama / History and General Background
CHRONOLOGY OF IMPORTANT HISTORICAL AND THEATRI-
CAL EVENTS   147
Greece / Rome
INDEX   153

ILLUSTRATIONS

Sketch Map of Ancient Greece 2
Pottery Bell-Krater of Dionysus, Maenads, and Satyrs 4
Attic Hydra Kalpis Vase Painting of Satyrs and Flute Player 13
Vase Painting of Poet Demetrius and Satyr-Play Actors 14
Drawings from Pronomos Vase of Satyr-Play Costumes and Masks 15
Vase Painting of Revelers Dressed as Birds 17
Terra-Cotta Statuette of Old Comedy Drunkards 21
Terra-Cotta Statuettes of Middle Comedy Actors, One with Food Basket 23
Ground Plan of Theatre of Thorikos 30
Reconstruction of Theatre of Dionysus and Temple 31
Reconstructions of Possible Scene Buildings in Theatre of Dionysus 32
Ground Plan of Section of Theatre of Dionysus 34
Ground Plan of Precinct of Dionysus Eleuthereus 35
Ground Plan of Theatre of Epidauros 37
Three Views of Ruins of Theatre of Epidauros 38
Reconstruction of Section of Hellenistic Theatre of Oropus 39
View of Ruins of Theatre of Priene 42
Reconstruction of Theatre of Priene 43
Reconstruction of Hellenistic Theatre at Delos 44
Production of Euripides' *Heracleidae* by Greek National Theatre 47

Production of Sophocles' *The Women of Trachis* by Greek National Theatre   47
Terra-Cotta Comic Mask and Tragic Mask, Hellenistic Period   61
Relief of Hellenistic Masks and Menander   61
Vase Painting of Euripides' Lost Play *Andromeda*   63
Terra-Cotta Statuette of Old Comedy Angry Old Man   64
Terra-Cotta Statuettes of Middle Comedy Actors, Woman and Man   64
Three Views of Bronze Statuette of Atellan-Farce Character Dossenus   74
Drawing from *Phlyake* Vase Painting   78
Terra-Cotta Statuettes of *Fabula Praetexta* Actors   81
Phlyake Vase Painting of Cheiron   89
Phlyake Vase Painting of Ares and Hephaestus Fighting before Hera   89
Reconstruction of "Plautine-Terentine" Stage   92
Ground Plan and Reconstruction of Theatre of Pompey   95
Section of Exterior of Theatre of Marcellus before Restoration   97
Ground Plan of Theatre of Marcellus   97
Ground Plan of Theatre of Magnesia as Classical and Hellenistic Theatre   99
Ground Plan of Theatre of Magnesia as Greco-Roman Theatre   100
Ground Plan and Cross-Section of a Theatre according to Vitruvius   102
Reconstruction of Theatre of Ostia after Enlargement   104
Partial Ground Plan of Theatre of Orange and Adjacent Circus   105
Reconstruction of Theatre of Orange Showing Its *Porticus*   106
Reconstruction of Theatre of Orange Showing *Scaenae Frons,* Orchestra, and Seating Area   106
Roman Comic Actors on Cover of Praenestine Cista   113
Relief Showing Roman Comedy Masks   116
Marble Copies of Roman Tragic Masks   116
Marble Statuette of Roman Comedy Slave   117
Ivory Statuette of Roman Tragic Actor   117
Ivory Relief of Female Pantomimist   121
Front and Back Views of Metal Statuette of Female Mime   122
Large Theatre at Pompeii   124
Ground Plan of Circus Maximus   129
Reconstruction of Circus of Nero   131
Terra-Cotta Plaque of Charioteer   132
View of Ruins of Colosseum   135

Exterior and Interior Reconstruction of Colosseum   136
Reconstruction of a *Venatione*   139
Amphitheatres at Capua and Pozzuoli   140
Reconstructions of Naumachiae Constructed by Domitian and
    Nero   142

PREFACE

This book is devoted to a historical account of the theatre in ancient Greece and Rome. It is basically centered on the concept of theatre as a performing art. Attention is focused on the origins and development of Greek and Roman dramatic offerings, on the theatres where they were given, and on the processes of production. In the case of the Romans, their games and spectacles are treated since these forms were so closely intertwined with the entire field of entertainment. Wherever possible, consideration is given to the theatre in relationship to the social and political fabric of the times.

I doubt that this book would ever have been written had it not been for the late Alan Downer of Princeton University who stimulated and encouraged me and gave many valuable suggestions during the early stages of its preparation. I am most indebted to him.

I wish to express my gratitude to several others who have contributed in the final preparation of this book. The editors, Professors Dunbar H. Ogden and Alois M. Nagler, have been most helpful with their criticisms. I am very grateful to Martha Kaufman for her drawings and to Vivian Joyce for typing the manuscript. I would also like to acknowledge all the individuals and publishers who so kindly gave their permission to reproduce the copyrighted materials.

The Theatre and Drama of Greece and Rome

1

GREEK DRAMA: ORIGIN AND DEVELOPMENT

Greek drama was born in the sixth century B.C., but it is plain, from surviving evidence, that other peoples and earlier cultures participated in activities involving dramatic elements—for example, the Coronation Festival Play and the Abydos Passion Play of the Egyptians. None, however, became a viable theatre production capable of existing on its own as part of an institution known as "theatre," whereas Greek drama did. It was a creation of great magnitude and imagination, far-reaching in its consequences; dance, song, and literature (in dialogue form) were welded together into an artistic construct that presented men who publicly acted out situations and characters based upon the lives of men and gods.

The ingenious processes which created the various forms of Greek drama—all the forces in operation—will perhaps never be fully understood. The present approach emphasizes the social and artistic climate that helped bring these new forms into being, the various steps or leaps taken, and the innovators and their materials. One thing is sure: It all seems to have happened very quickly.

Drama first developed during the age of the Greek tyrants (650–500 B.C.), when the city-states, stimulated by trade and population growth, moved rapidly toward greater urbanization. Greek tyrants were similar in many ways to our modern dictators—highly autocratic, but strong execu-

1

Sketch map of ancient Greece; several of these important centers were associated with early theatrical developments. (Drawing by Martha Kaufman.)

tives.[1] They were usually placed in power by the newly emerging middle class, which consisted of businessmen who tried to break the stranglehold of the landowning aristocrats who controlled them. Fortunately, most of the tyrants worked to make their cities stronger economically as well as better places in which their subjects could live. They fostered civic building programs that furnished needed employment and, at the same time, helped to beautify the cities. A few of the tyrants were highly cultured and turned their attention to the arts. Their direct aid and interest in the theatre, and in the other performing arts closely associated with it, were extremely important. Periander, tyrant of Corinth in the sixth century B.C.

(ca. 625–585 B.C.), who made Corinth one of the great cities of antiquity, had as his guest Arion of Lesbos. Arion revolutionized the improvised dithyrambs (*dithyrambos*, a narrative hymn honoring Dionysus sung and danced by a chorus consisting of a leader and his followers) by writing them out, trained choruses to perform within a prescribed area, and finally instituted discipline and order into what had been a highly informal type of revel. In several of his dithyrambs, Arion even had the chorus members dressed as satyrs while they imitated some of the satyrs' actions. Cleisthenes, sixth-century tyrant of Sicyon, transferred the *tragikoi choroi* (goat dances) of his city from a worship of Adrastus, a legendary king, to Dionysus. He called upon Epigenes to reshape the dances and songs and make them more artistic. Epigenes may have reached out and used the adventures of mythic heroes as well as those of Dionysus—a practice followed at the later Dionysian festivals in Athens.[2] Pisistratus, the famous enlightened tyrant of Athens, went the farthest of all. He increased the splendor of the Panathenaea (the universal festival of all Athens dedicated to Athena), and he established the festival known as the Greater Dionysia, or City Dionysia, around 534 B.C. to honor the popular god Dionysus.[3] It featured the performance of tragedy, an innovation at the time.

The almost unbelievable Athenian victories at Marathon in 490 B.C., and the naval victory at Salamis in 480 B.C., suddenly thrust Athens into prominence. It appears highly unreasonable to accept as mere coincidence the fact that Greek drama was primarily Athenian drama and that Greece's victory over Persia was primarily an Athenian victory. Athens became the focal point of power and prestige in Greece; after these victories she was able to maintain her prominence during an extended period of relative peace and stability. It was during this propitious time that Greek drama developed and flourished. With the fall of Athens, in 404 B.C., this remarkable period of creativity ceased.

Formative materials for tragedy and satyr drama are to be found in the dithyrambs and/or *rhapsōidia* (recitation of narrative epic poems of Homer). For comedy, these materials are to be found in phallic (fertility) songs, mumming revels (persons wearing disguises or masks and merrymaking), Doric farces (crude improvised sketches or playlets), and other festive happenings. These will all be considered when the probable origins of each type of Greek drama are discussed. The dithyramb, however, merits special consideration for its influence as a seminal force in the development of drama.

DITHYRAMBS

The dithyramb was introduced into Greece with the religious cult of Dionysus, which had originated in Asia Minor.[4] The worship of Dionysus bordered on ecstatic frenzy, particularly on the part of his closest followers. These included men who impersonated satyrs (half-human and half-goat or half-horse), sileni (elderly drunken satyrs), and women maenads or bacchantes (frenzied women). In early periods, the Dionysian revelers danced and sang in wild, drunken abandon on the lonely sides of mountains, and in their fervor they would tear animals to pieces and eat them as part of their ceremonies. Dionysus, their leader, was associated with fertility rites, growth (the birth and the death cycle), and especially with the grape vines. The dithyrambs honored this newer god and were no doubt tamed by the time they reached the City Dionysia festival in approximately 510 B.C. A wide range of subjects relating to Dionysus was

Red-figured pottery bell-krater, attributed to Methyse painter (ca. 450 B.C.), of Dionysus, holding a cup, and his followers, maenads and satyrs. (Courtesy, The Metropolitan Museum of Art, Rogers Fund [1907].)

available for dithyrambs, including his miraculus birth and other spectacular events in his life. In addition, stories of early Greek heroes were often used; further improvements in dancing and music were made; and a standardized chorus of 50 members was established.

The dithyramb was apparently a dynamic, flexible, fast-changing, and immensely popular form of entertainment during the sixth century B.C. Moreover, its popularity increased in the fifth and fourth centuries B.C. While the dithyramb continued to develop its independent life, it directly influenced the creation of satyr drama and may have done the same for tragedy.

TRAGEDIES

Thespis, of whom little is known, is the subject of much controversy when it comes to discerning the specific part he played in the origins of tragedy. A sixth-century B.C. resident of the Athenian deme (district) of Icaria, the present-day town of Dionyso located a few miles west of the site of the Battle of Marathon, Thespis is credited by several ancient writers with the invention of tragedy. How he accomplished this feat lies at the heart of the mystery surrounding the birth of tragedy and will most likely never be known, for too many clues are missing. The most commonly held theory is based upon Aristotle's statement that "Tragedy—as also Comedy—was at first mere improvisation. The one originated with the authors of the Dithyramb, the other with those of the phallic songs, which are still in use in many of our cities."[5] According to this theory, Thespis would have begun with some form of the dithyramb (similar to the improvised forms Arion had reworked in Corinth), widened the subject matter by drawing upon Homeric legends, added an actor (himself), a written prologue, and spoken verse (which he delivered). No longer trusting improvisation, he scored the songs of the chorus and choreographed their dancing.

Thespis assumed a character, impersonating an epic hero, and the chorus (perhaps as many as 50 members) and its leader reacted to his sufferings. This action on the part of Thespis—assuming a character other than himself, substituting it for his own personality, expressing the feelings and thoughts of this imagined character to others publicly and in turn reacting to their feelings and ideas—was a crucial step forward. *This was the inventive act needed to create tragedy.*

To summarize this theory, it can be assumed that Thespis, in establishing tragedy, drew upon dance, music, epic tales, dithyrambs, lyric poetry, and—most importantly—impersonation. To facilitate his impersonation, he first used white lead to paint his face; later he used a linen mask.

Else maintains that instead of looking to the dithyramb and its choral leaders for the roots of tragedy, attention should be focused on the *rhap-sōidia* contests, for they eventually led to the invention of tragedy.[6] These contests were held at the Panathenaea festival and dated from about 566 B.C., when they were started by Solon. Reciters delivered portions of *The Iliad* and *The Odyssey*. Later, Pisistratus established the City Dionysia around 534 B.C. to celebrate Dionysus, who was by then the common man's god. This festival featured tragedy, a new genre created by Thespis in which he directly impersonated an epic hero, rather than utilizing the quasi-impersonations formerly used by the rhapsodists. The hero's "pathos" was the center of Thespian tragedy, and the chorus, which linked spectators with his suffering, was added to furnish a "sounding board for the heroic passion." Kitto agrees with Else on this last point and says that "the originality of Thespis consisted not in his adding something histrionic to a chorus, but a chorus to something histrionic."[7]

Else states that tragedy was a uniquely Athenian invention based on "a sequence of two creative leaps by Thespis and Aeschylus, with certain conditioning factors precedent to each" and that it was *not in essence Dionysiac* and that it did not emerge from any religious cult. Else further believes that *tragōidos* (*tragos* goat, *aeidein* to sing), goat singer, linguistically pertained to the poet-actor, the reciter of verses who was so named because originally a "tragedian" was awarded a goat as a prize. Since Thespis was the first *tragōidos,* he invented *tragōidia* (tragedy).

The puzzlement over the exact parentage of Greek tragedy will no doubt continue, and more theories may be forthcoming. Someone may revive the question by turning back to other mystery rites of ancient Greece—such as the Eleusinian mysteries, the vegetation rituals, or the cult of the dead (hero-cult)—and giving them new interpretations and relationships to account for the birth of tragedy, for each of these has had vociferous advocates in the past.[8]

In performance, early Greek tragedies consisted of a series of acted episodes performed by one soliloquizing actor who also conversed with the leader of a chorus. During this action, chorus members reacted in patterned movements and gestures to what was happening in the orchestra (circular space in front of the proscenium from *orcheisthai* to dance). Between episodes the chorus danced, recited in recitative, and sang choral odes that related to past events or foreshadowed what was about to happen. It was possible for a single actor, by changing his mask and costume during a choral ode and reappearing before the audience as another character, to play more than one role. Doubling and tripling in roles was a common practice. Later, a second, then a third actor were added —never more. There were always more characters than actors to play them.

Stories based on the Trojan War, as derived from Homer and other sources now lost, as well as selected recent historical events such as the Persian Wars, furnished tragic playwrights with dramatic materials. These they handled by freely interpreting the materials to suit their individual purposes.

About 35 years separate the official beginning of tragedy in Athens by Thespis from the start of Aeschylus' writing career. The three known playwrights during this period, aside from Thespis, were Choerilus, Phrynichus, and Pratinas. A native Athenian, Choerilus came into prominence around 525 B.C., continued writing into the fifth century, competed with Aeschylus, authored 160 plays, and won 13 contests. Phrynichus won his first victory around 511/8 B.C. The subjects of a few of his plays, namely *Alcestis* and *The Danaids*, were used by later dramatists. *The Fall of Miletus* and *The Phoenician Women* were based on contemporary events. He did not restrict himself to Dionysian material, but drew on a wide range of sources. It has been said that his choruses initiated new dance steps and movements. Pratinas, the inventor of satyr drama, is credited with writing 18 tragedies, of which very little is known. In summary, scattered fragments, a few titles, and a limited number of comments by ancient writers are all the documentation there is for sixth-century Athenian drama.

The fifth century was the most productive era for Greek tragedy. It coincided with and reflected Athens' burgeoning rise to greatness as a center for intellectual discovery, artistic development, religious worship, and political enlightenment. Fortunately for Athens, her playwrights were able to capture some of this ferment.

Of the total estimated output of fifth-century tragedies, 31, or about 3 per cent, have survived, and most judgments of Greek tragedy are based on them. They, in turn, represent only a small portion of the total dramatic works of three playwrights—Aeschylus, Sophocles, and Euripides.

AESCHYLUS

The earliest of the surviving Greek plays are those of Aeschylus (525/4–456 B.C.), who was one of the theatre's most important innovators. Tragedy underwent its greatest development and change during his career as a practicing playwright (499–456 B.C.), and especially after 470 B.C. He was the true creator of tragedy as it is known today. The son of an aristocrat, Aeschylus was born at Eleusis, site of the famous mysteries. During his boyhood and early manhood, he witnessed Athens establish equality for its citizens before the law and saw Athens hold off its external enemies. Later, he fought in the battles of Marathon and Salamis, where the Persians were decisively defeated. These victories made it possible for Greece, in an atmosphere of freedom, to develop her intellectual and artistic life.

About 90 plays are reputed to have been written by Aeschylus; titles for 82 are known, but only seven survive: *The Persians* (ca. 472 B.C.); *Seven Against Thebes* (467 B.C.); *The Oresteia* (458 B.C.), the only extant Greek trilogy, consisting of *Agamemnon, The Libation Bearers*, and *The Eumenides*; *The Suppliant Maidens* (ca. 463 B.C.?), and *Prometheus Bound* (ca. 460 B.C.?). These plays belong to the last 16 years of his career, his most productive and experimental period. Aeschylus won his first victory in 484 B.C., and he accumulated 13 prizes in all. This means that 52 of his plays, or more than half his entire output, were of winning caliber. Tragic playwrights competed at the City Dionysia for prizes and were judged on the basis of four plays they furnished as a group—three tragedies and one satyr play—rather than on single plays.

Aeschylus added a second actor, which helped broaden and deepen the tragic action, for even as a messenger or herald this actor could vitally alter a hero's position with the type of news he conveyed. Furthermore, this addition of the second actor tended to reduce the importance of the chorus.

The prolonged and bitter Persian Wars and the extended sufferings of the Athenians deeply affected Aeschylus and probably led him to the trilogic structuring of his later plays. In linking by theme three separate plays—by creating trilogies—he was able to gain greater scope and breadth, to probe human choices, to dwell on the resultant suffering due to the workings of divine justice. The three plays comprising *The Oresteia* gave him the means to examine on a broad scale the evils of the Trojan War, the crime of Clytemnestra murdering her husband and of Orestes murdering his mother, and the manner by which the gods eventually helped to bring order out of such chaos. Man, according to Aeschylus, learns through suffering, which eventually leads to understanding and to wisdom. The dramaturgy in *The Oresteia* was further improved by a third actor, presumably introduced earlier by Sophocles and adopted by Aeschylus.

SOPHOCLES

Sophocles (497/6–406 B.C.), almost 30 years younger than Aeschylus and 12 years older than Euripides, was born in the deme (district) of Coloneus, near Athens, of wealthy parents who provided him with an excellent education. His productive years as a dramatist were spent during the zenith of Athenian culture. He died just two years before the fall of Athens. According to Plutarch, Sophocles' first victory came in 468 B.C., when he defeated Aeschylus with plays so impressive that the archon (presiding officer) bypassed the usual judging system and called upon the council of generals to decide the winner. Sophocles was victorious at the City Dionysia 18 times as well as winning six victories at the Lenaea, ancient Athens' other major festival which featured comedy and included tragedy. The total of his plays is given as 123; titles for 114 are known, but only seven are extant: *Ajax* (442 B.C.), *Antigone* (ca. 441 B.C.), *Oedipus the King* (ca. 430 B.C.), *The Trachinian Women* (ca. 413 B.C.), *Philoctetes* (409 B.C.), *Electra* (ca. 410 B.C.), and *Oedipus at Coloneus* (406 B.C.). A greater part of *The Ichneutai* (*The Trackers*), a satyr play, has been preserved. These plays cover a span of roughly 40 years, a much better temporal distribution than for any of the other tragic playwrights. His last play, *Oedipus at Coloneus*, was produced posthumously in 401 B.C.

The surviving works indicate clearly Sophocles' great skill and craftsmanship in plotting, handling exposition, employing dramatic irony, effectively using divination (oracles and soothsayers), revealing characters by their reactions to changing situations, and adroitly using and motivating characters' exits and entrances. Greatest of all his achievements was *Oedipus the King*, a flawless play in every respect and the model Aristotle drew upon to illustrate Greek tragedy at its best.

Early in his career, Sophocles abandoned the practice of writing trilogies. This is mentioned by Suidas (tenth-century A.D. Greek who compiled a dictionary of his predecessors), and has been confirmed by an inscription bearing the name of one of the Sophoclean trilogies. By making each of his later plays into complete, tight, compact, self-contained units, he was able to focus attention more directly on the tragic hero than had Aeschylus. Sophocles added a third actor, which made it possible for him to construct more complex plots, reveal more nuances of character, and reduce the role of the chorus.

In Sophoclean tragedy, the ways of the gods are not always revealed to man; rather, his existence is constantly threatened. Creon's action in *Antigone*, when he fails to perceive the unwritten laws of the gods and makes unjust and evil decisions, brings disaster to himself and all those dearest to him—his wife, son, and niece.

A lost document by Sophocles, *On the Chorus*, is reputed to have mentioned his increasing the tragic chorus from 12 to 15 members.

Sophocles acted in his younger days; he later gave it up, probably because acting was becoming more specialized and good actors were available.

EURIPIDES

The first contest in which Euripides (485/4–406 B.C.) was granted a chorus and given a chance to compete with a group of his plays occurred in 455 B.C. One of his four entries was *Peliades*, an early treatment of the Medea story. However, it was not until 441 B.C. that he won the first prize. He was to win four more, one of which was awarded after his death with the extant *Iphigenia in Aulis*, *The Bacchae*, and the lost *Alcmaeon at Corinth*. Of Euripides' total output of about 88 plays, 17 tragedies and one satyr play, *The Cyclops* (ca. 423 B.C.), are extant. Included among the surviving tragedies are *Alcestis* (438 B.C.), *Medea* (431 B.C.), *Hippolytus* (428 B.C.), *The Heracleidae* (ca. 424 B.C.), *Andromache* (ca. 426 B.C.), *Hecuba* (ca. 425 B.C.), *Heracles* (ca. 422 B.C.), *The Suppliants* (ca. 421 B.C.), *Ion* (ca. 417 B.C.), *The Trojan Women* (415 B.C.), *Electra* (ca. 413 B.C.), *Iphigenia in Tauris* (ca. 414/2 B.C.), *Helen* (412 B.C.), *The Phoenician Women* (ca. 409 B.C.), *Orestes* (408 B.C.), *The Bacchae* (ca. 405 B.C.), and *Iphigenia in Aulis* (ca. 405 B.C.). These plays are all products of his last 32 years. Euripides' popularity was much greater after his death—especially in the rather skeptical thought of the fourth century B.C.—than during his lifetime, and it is for this reason that so many of his plays have survived.

The principal changes in tragedy instituted by Euripides dealt with form, the choice of subject matter, the treatment of characters, and the intellectual and philosophical content. These were the areas his contemporaries criticized.

He often resorted to prologues for exposition, probably because it was the easiest way of getting needed background information to an audience. Sometimes it was effective; the opening prologue of *The Bacchae* is a good example for it "fits" the play. To resolve plots, Euripides frequently introduced the *deus ex machina* (the god from the machine). In *Iphigenia in Tauris*, Athena's sudden appearance via the *mēchanē* (a crane used to fly actors) near the end of the play enabled Euripides to reestablish the connection with the cult whose gods had become irrelevant and eventually subservient to skeptics and sophists and to the inner structure and meaning of his play. A *mēchanē* drawn by dragons was used by Medea in the play bearing her name when, with the bodies of her dead children, she made her final spectacular escape from Jason. Euripides' love of rhetoric, no doubt a reflection of his concern for the philosophical and ethical questioning that was being voiced by teachers and philosophers of his day, found its way into his plays by his use of the elements of formal, balanced debate —for example, the rhetorical arguments between Jason and Medea. This particular part of his work, though sharply questioned at the time, was praised by later generations.

Euripides was frequently attracted by extremes when choosing subject matter and characters. He was concerned about the morbid and abnormal qualities of such people as Orestes, Phaedra, and Medea, for he felt that it was part of a playwright's task to treat every type of material. They fitted into the skeptics' probing, questioning attack on all issues and people that was making itself felt in Athens at the time. The pathetic, the sentimental, and the melodramatic also had an appeal for Euripides, and he frequently exploited children for these purposes.

The intellectual climate of Athens during the second half of the fifth century was heavily influenced by the sophists, led by Protagoras and Prodicus. These men advocated that "man was the measure of all things," that truth was relative to each man's outlook, that men could not tell whether gods do or do not exist, and that everything—any question—was open to debate: The crosscurrents of doubt generated by the sophists had a profound effect on Euripides and his works, for it is said that he studied under its leading advocates and absorbed some of their ideas. As a result, in Euripidean drama, man's choices are not necessarily geared to the workings of divine justice and his resultant suffering does not lead to his gaining wisdom, in the Aeschylean sense. Nor is man's existence constantly threatened, because the ways of the gods are not revealed to him, as in Sophoclean drama. Rather, man's destiny basically evolves out of himself and his own control or lack of control of his passions. Medea and Phaedra are good examples of Euripidean tragic figures caught in the fierce whirlpools of human passion. It is this quality that makes Euripides a modern and sets him apart from Aeschylus and Sophocles.

Euripides further reduced the importance of the chorus and brought the actors into still greater prominence. This was a continuing trend which was accelerated during the fourth century.

TRAGEDIES AFTER EURIPIDES

All that may be firmly established about postclassical tragedy, with our limited evidence, are some general trends. *The Rhesus*, based on the Tenth

Book of *The Iliad*, is the only surviving tragedy. Its author, as well as its exact date, is unknown. Not much can be drawn from it that would be of help in explaining the tragedies written during this period. From some of the extant titles, we learn that there were plays which dealt with the stories of Adonis, Cinyras, and Phereae. This suggests that mythical subjects not previously used in plays made their appearance in fourth- and third-century tragedies. The increased interest in rhetoric that grew out of the sophist movement, the greater concern for individual psychological characterizations that stemmed from the works of Euripides, the newer trends in music and dance that were developing—all of these found their way into the tragedies.

As Hellenic culture spread, and as each city began to have its own theatre, the writing of tragedies was no longer limited solely to Athens. Acting assumed much greater importance. It was the direct result of greater specialization and better actor training. The actor's work soon overshadowed that of the playwrights. The revival of classical tragedies, that began about 386 B.C. and continued thereafter, also focused more attention on the actors.

STRUCTURE OF A TRAGEDY

Structurally, Greek tragedies tend to follow the same general pattern. Usually they open with a prologue (consisting of a dialogue or monologue scene) which sets the exposition. The opening scene in *Antigone* between the two sisters, Antigone and Ismene, is illustrative of a most effective opening dialogue scene. This is followed by the *parodos*, in which the chorus enters singing or chanting in recitative, which reinforces the exposition and sets the emotional tone of the play. *The Persians*, the earliest surviving play, begins immediately with the *parodos* and omits the prologue section. This may have been a throwback to Thespian tragedies. After the *parodos* come the episodes, in which the actions of the plays are depicted by the characters. Each episode is separated from the next by a *stasimon* (choral song). Most extant Greek tragedies have five episodes, though *Oedipus the King* has six. The last *stasimon* provides the closing scene as the chorus and actors depart.

Greek tragic playwrights derived their subjects from legendary epic tales or historical events, changed them to suit their purposes, and made them theatrically effective. The characters in the plays tended to be few in number. The action was usually brief and dealt only with the climactic part of a story or event. Normally, killings and other violence occurred off-stage and were reported by messengers.

SATYR PLAYS

Satyr dramas were related to tragedies in two ways. They resembled them in general form, although they dealt with grotesque sections of Greek legendary material surrounding Dionysus. And they were written by tragic playwrights.

It is thought that satyr dramas were a late offshoot of the dithyrambs, heavily influenced by tragedies. They utilized a chorus costumed as satyrs (the woodland attendants of Dionysus), who were endowed with special fertility powers. They were lusty, bestial, wanton forest creatures equipped with horse tails or goat legs and bristling animallike ears and hair. Satyrs participated in many of the early dithyrambs, but it is impossible to discover the form of their participation or their influence on the embryonic stages of Greek tragedy. Since these satyr performers impersonated and disguised themselves as creatures other than themselves, one could safely assume that this was assuredly a definite step in the direction

Attic red-figured hydra kalpis, detail of shoulder, Bacchie scene; vase painting of dancing satyrs, accompanied by a bearded flute player, assembling a couch. (03.788, Courtesy, Museum of Fine Arts, Boston.)

Vase painting (late 5th cent. B.C.) of poet Demetrius, Dionysus, actors, chorus members, and flute player (Pronomos), all connected with satyr play possibly entitled *Hesione.* (National Museum, Naples. Photo Alinari.)

of creating a dramatic form. Supposedly, as tragedy developed, this cruder form of entertainment was forced into the background.

Suidas states that Pratinas of Phlius (an ancient village located in the northern section of the Peloponnesus between Sicyon and Argos), a contemporary of Aeschylus, invented satyr drama by employing a chorus of satyrs based upon prototypes used in earlier dithyrambs and by introducing suitable characters to fit the subject matter of the plays. In all, Pratinas wrote 50 plays, of which 32 were satyr dramas, and he was victorious once. There are one or two other references to him, but they are not very helpful.

Flickinger has indicated that satyr drama came into being because tragedies had lost their "Bacchic themes" and that a certain proportion of the audience demanded a return to plays containing these themes.[9] Satyr drama fitted this concept with its strong emphasis on mythological burlesque. Sometime between 534 and 501 B.C., when the City Dionysia was reorganized, satyr plays were incorporated into the program and presented as the fourth play furnished by each tragic playwright, in addition to his three tragedies.

A number of vase paintings depicting satyrs and sileni (elderly satyrs) and two extant satyr plays are the primary source materials for studying satyr dramas. Unfortunately, with few exceptions, the vase paintings do not depict theatrical scenes. The few that do date after 450 B.C. indicate that theatrical satyrs were evidently a combination of the caprine (goat satyrs from the Peloponnesus) and the equine (horse) sileni conventionalized to a degree. They were provided with horse ears and tails, loincloths often painted to represent goat skins, human feet, and were hornless.

One of the extant satyr plays is *The Cyclops*, written by Euripides about 423 B.C. This play is based on an episode from the Ninth Book of *The Odyssey*, relating the meeting of Odysseus on the slopes of Mount Etna in Sicily with the giant cyclops Polyphemus and a captive band of satyrs led by old Silenus. Euripides, in adapting this story for the stage, cut the action to a single day, omitted the huge stone used to close the mouth of the cave, changed Odysseus and his followers' method of escape from the cave, and used only one cyclops.

The other extant satyr play, *The Ichneutai* (*The Trackers*), was written by Sophocles about 440 B.C. The papyrus containing the play's mutilated text, ending at Line 439, was discovered in Egypt in 1911. Using *The*

Drawings from Pronomos vase of costumes and masks worn in satyr plays. (From Baumeister, *Denkmaler des Klassischen Altertums*, Vol. II [1889].)

Homeric Hymn to Hermes as his main source, Green reconstructed Lines 440 to 750.[10] The play is concerned with Apollo's search for his missing herd of cows stolen by the six-day-old Hermes, inventor of the lyre.

OLD COMEDY

Following the clues given by Aristotle, one can trace Old Comedy (ca. 565–404 B.C.) to the leaders of the songs of phallic processions and to Aristotle's statement that "The claim to Comedy is put forward by the Megarians—not only by those of Greece proper, who allege that it originated under their democracy, but also by the Megarians of Sicily, for the poet Epicharmus, who is much earlier than Chionides and Magnes, belonged to that country."[11] The word "comedy" stems from *kōmōidia* (*kōmos* revel, *aeidein* to sing), the song of revelers. Initial attention, then, should be directed to phallic rites and other associated revels and ultimately to the Megarian or Doric mimes as they are frequently called.

The salient part of the Dionysian cult worship was expressed by choruses moving in processions. And since fertility (agricultural, animal, and human) was the basis of this specific worship, the phallus (penis), the male symbol of fertility, was a necessary element. The simplest procession consisted of a chorus, its leaders garlanded with ivy and flowers, singing appropriate songs, and moving in rhythmic patterns. The procession was led by a flute player. Chorus members carried large phallic symbols on poles. In some of the processions improvised abuses and obscenities were hurled back and forth between chorus members and onlookers, supposedly adding to the magical powers of the rites.

The legendary Susarion, an Icarian, led choral performances consisting of iambic invectives of personal mockery between about 581 and 560 B.C. These were first given in the marketplace of his native village and later in Athens. It was also in Icaria that Thespis performed his earliest experimental work which led to the creation of tragedy. This village was also responsible for introducing Dionysian worship into Attica.

Other types of *kōmoi* popular in many parts of ancient Greece were those featuring revelers dressed in animal costumes, particularly headdresses of animals. These mumming revels and phallic processions lacked such definite dramatic elements, however, as plot and individual personation, which would have been necessary to transmute them into plays. Nevertheless, they did involve chanting and singing by a number of followers in the processions as well as group personation—both basic ingredients of a dramatic chorus.

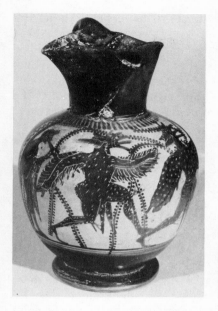

Black-figured vase painting (6th cent. B.C.) of revelers or dancers dressed as birds, with feathered wings and heads. Later Aristophanes employed a chorus of birds in his play *The Birds.* (Courtesy, Trustees of the British Museum.)

Doric mimes (*mimos,* akin to *mimeisthai* to imitate) were another branch of very early comedy, nonchoral in nature, that heavily influenced Old Comedy in its formative phases. They originated in an important center for Doric culture, Megara, located 27 miles southwest of Athens, during its democracy (ca. 581–424 B.C.). Doric mimes appeared at about the same time that Susarion was staging comic choral performances in Icaria. At first they were improvised, but later they were written down. The term was interchangeably applied to both actors and plays. Figures on sixth-century B.C. Corinthian vases depict mime actors wearing short, heavily underpadded costumes (sometimes padded both front and back); several are equipped with masks and huge phalluses. There are references to Megarian mimes in *The Acharnians* and *The Wasps* of Aristophanes. Terracotta figurines of mime actors, together with the fragments of later, written mime sketches, which began appearing with the work of Epicharmus (sixth century B.C.), Sophron (fifth century B.C.), and Herodas[12] and Theoritus (third century B.C.), furnish scholars with the basic information for reconstructing this type of theatrical entertainment.[13]

Story material and stock characters for Doric mimes came from two general sources: mythology acted out in burlesque fashion, and comic intrigues drawn from daily life and treated in a manner close to the general public's earthy interests. In their earliest years they were handled by improvisational techniques but gained literary status very early in the fifth century B.C.

The ancient mimes (players) who gave "imitations of life" were skilled at more than character and situation portrayal. They also effectively imitated animals and birds, a feature present in many of the later Old Comedies. Dancing, singing, acrobatics, and juggling were among the important skills possessed by these versatile mime performers and were incorporated into their performances.

Epicharmus (ca. 530–ca. 440 B.C.), the Sicilian Doric poet, was the first to give literary form to short, nonchoral comic sketches (mimes) burlesquing myths. In others, he parodied some of the facets of the contemporary philosophical thinking. He is credited with introducing character types into his works—parasites, drunkards, and many others. No doubt these short playlets had a decided effect upon Old Comedy during its formative years, as they showed comedy writers how to focus the action of their plays more on individuals (actors) rather than depending entirely upon a chorus.

Farther south in the Peloponnesus, in the vicinity of Sparta, there existed another type of improvised mimic farce which influenced Old Comedy. The discovery of clay masks and evidence furnished by Sosibius (a fourth-century B.C. writer) are the principal sources dealing with this branch of mime. They were performed by *deikelistai* (masked characters) acting several parts, including slaves, foolish doctors, a witchlike woman or old-hag type, a ruddy-faced, bald-headed glutton, and others.

To sum up, Old Comedy drew upon phallic processions with leaders improvising songs and dialogue, various mumming revels, improvised Doric mimes from Megara and Sparta, and the special variety skills interjected into these mimes by performers. All were blended into a loose structural form of entertainment that was highly satirical, allegorical, and farcical.

In 501 B.C., when the *kōmos* was made an official part of the City Dionysia, it consisted of a chorus of animals or birds featuring an entrance song *(parodos)* and a ritualistic fight or conflict *(agōn)* between half-choruses and their leaders. The chorus then spoke as a body to the audience *(parabasis)* in a humorous way, verbally attacking various political matters, social problems, and prominent individuals. The finish was marked by some type of spirited exodus.

Comedies were finally officially recognized—that is, granted a chorus at the City Dionysia—in 487/6 B.C., two years before Aeschylus won his first prize. They lagged far behind tragedies in their development and remained longer in the free improvisational state. The intellectual awakening that occurred in Greece during the fifth century was the impetus that finally gave form to comedy. Chionides, who won the first official contest in 486 B.C., and Magnes, with his victory in 472 B.C. (the first of 11 such victories), are hardly more than names to us today. Contests for comic poets began at the Lenaea, Athens' other great dramatic festival, in 432 B.C.

The peak period for Old Comedy was 450–404 B.C., when Athens was organizing and establishing its empire, solidifying itself as the center of commerce and trade in the Hellenic world, and launching a huge civic building program on the Acropolis. It was a time of intellectual excitement and skepticism as well as of artistic achievement. Athens, with a citizen population of approximately 60,000 and an over-all population of 155,000, was moving constitutionally in a more democratic direction, thus creating greater possibilities for its poorer citizens to hold government offices. The skeptics' skill in public speaking, dialectics, and the manipulation of people's minds was increasing and causing concern in several quarters. The last 30 years of the fifth century witnessed the devastating Peloponnesian War, which broke out in 431 B.C. between Sparta and Athens and was only suspended briefly during the short Peace of Nicias in 421–418 B.C., reached its climax in the disastrous defeat of the Athenians in the Sicilian Expedition of 415–413 B.C. and ended with the final siege and surrender of Athens in 404 B.C.

The comic poet Cratinus (ca. 490–ca. 420 B.C.), who wrote 21 comedies, nine of which won first prizes (the first was in 453 B.C.), and Crates, a contemporary and author of about eight comedies (three of them first-prize winners), gave much needed order and substance to Old Comedy. Cratinus was regarded by critics and students of antiquity as the first to develop political comedy. In this genre he attacked the policies of Pericles and his associates and directed scorn toward the leading sophists. His play, *The Wine-Flask*, was victorious in 423 B.C., defeating *The Connos* by Ameipsias and *The Clouds* by Aristophanes. A papyrus fragment of *Dionysalexandros* gives some idea of the skill of Cratinus in handling mythological burlesque as a popular subject for early comedy. Crates gave up lampooning and personal attacks and turned to more general subjects. Fragments (which are all we have) suggest that in *The Beasts* he used talking animals in the chorus, and in *The Neighbors* he introduced drunken men.

Eupolis (ca. 446–ca. 412 B.C.), a contemporary and rival of Aristophanes, wrote about 14 plays, seven of which won victories. *The Flatterers*, it may be noted, defeated Aristophanes' *Peace* in 421 B.C. Known titles of Eupolis' work also include *The Demes*, *The Brigadiers*, and *The*

Non-Combatants. His plays were noted for their charm, aptness of jokes, and imaginative qualities.[14]

The greatest master of Old Comedy was Aristophanes (ca. 445–ca. 388 B.C.), who wrote 40 plays, 11 of which are extant, together with several titles and numerous fragments from 26 of his lost plays. This material furnishes the most reliable, though limited, knowledge of Old Comedy. The extant plays are *The Acharnians* (425 B.C.), *The Knights* (424 B.C.), *The Clouds* (423 B.C.), *The Wasps* (422 B.C.), *Peace* (421 B.C.), *The Birds* (414 B.C.), *Lysistrata* (411 B.C.), *The Thesmophoriazusae* (411 B.C.), *The Frogs* (405 B.C.), *The Ecclesiazusae* (392/4 B.C.), and *Plutus* (388 B.C.).

Throughout his professional career Aristophanes was actively engaged with the issues and leaders of his day. Using the theatre as a forum for his satire, he publicly confronted both leaders and issues. Few problems or important persons escaped his attention. Obviously, war and peace concerned him greatly, for his adolescence was spent in the unsettled years foreshadowing the Peloponnesian War. This war was unleashed about the time he was nearing manhood and continued throughout most of his productive years. Three of Aristophanes' extant plays—*The Acharnians*, *Peace*, and *Lysistrata*—deal directly with ways peace might be achieved. The sex strike in *Lysistrata* suggested a most ingenious way of bringing men home from the battlefields. In *The Wasps* Aristophanes decried the abuses of the Athenian jury system and the harm it had done to the city's old men. The sophists, including Socrates and his students, were roundly castigated as corrupters of youth in *The Clouds*, for Aristophanes felt that their advocacy of a skeptical philosophy was of little help in the improvement of Athens, but contributed rather to its decadence. The demagogue Cleon was chastised in *The Knights*, and Euripides was unmercifully flayed in *The Frogs*. Both men were openly despised by Aristophanes, who felt that they were extremely dangerous—the former for his policies, and the latter for the destructive ideas expressed in his plays.

In Old Comedy there was a degree of freedom and frankness—a license in language, situations, and stage portrayal—difficult for us to realize fully, even today. It contained an incredible mixture of high and low comedy, satire, buffoonery, slapstick, verbal play, parody, allegory, metaphor, abuse, sex, caricature, invective, lampoon, singing, dancing, nudity, and vulgarity often in its crudest form. All of this information is based on the texts of Aristophanes' surviving comedies.

Structurally, Aristophanic comedy follows a loose pattern, the result of its mixed parentage. However, the general features of the plays remain fairly constant and within an identifiable framework—allowing, of course,

Terra-cotta statuette of Old Comedy drunkards
with padded costumes and grotesque grinning
masks having large mouth openings. (Courtesy,
State Museum of Berlin.)

for variations in each play. The plays usually begin with an expository
dialogue among the characters. In *The Wasps*, the slaves Sosias and
Xanthias converse while they guard Philocleon's house, which is surrounded by a huge net to prevent Philocleon from escaping and joining
his old jury friends at court. His son, Bdelycleon, is stationed on the roof
to ensure that his father, who is addicted to jury service and is happiest
when casting his ballots for convictions, does not escape through the

chimney. Occasionally, in the midst of one of Aristophanes' expository scenes, a character breaks off and speaks directly to the audience in prologue fashion and explains what he, the actor, is going to do to win audience favor, while also revealing relevant plot information. Xanthias does this when he abruptly turns to the audience and says, "I must explain the matter to the spectators" and then continues for 80 lines pointing out to the audience that he is not going to throw baskets of nuts to them, nor is he going to assail Euripides or belabor Cleon; rather he is trying to keep Philocleon from going to court and is going to attempt to cure him of his obsession for serving as a juror. This speech is followed by additional dialogue, and then the chorus of 24 old men, ex-soldiers and friends of Philocleon, dressed as wasps, make their entrance singing the *parodos* (entrance song). They have come to take Philocleon with them to court. Shortly after, an *agōn* (debate or contest) develops between Bdelycleon and Philocleon (the leading characters), with members of the chorus joining in the arguments. Eventually, they arrive at a "happy idea." Bdelycleon contends that his father should stay at home, establish his own court, and deal out justice to his slaves and other creatures around his house, rather than going to court each day. Soon the execution of the "happy idea" is set in motion when Labes, one of the household dogs, is apprehended, tried for stealing a Sicilian cheese, and acquitted by mistake —much to Philocleon's chagrin. Now, at last, Philocleon is freed from jury duty and convicting people and free to enjoy a life of pleasure. The actors leave the stage, and the chorus come forward in a *parabasis* to reproach the audience for ill-treating their playwright's works in the past and to remind them that the playwright has merely tried to purify their country and remove its evils. The chorus recall their own past heroism in battle and declare that they stand ready to act as wasps and sting their foes. The actors return to the stage, enact a series of ludicrous episodes in which Bdelycleon tries to teach his father how to be a gentleman and how really to enjoy life. A brief choral ode follows, during which interval Philocleon has been down town and cavorted outrageously, as he thinks a gentleman should. In the process he has gotten drunk, insulted a number of persons, and absconded with a nude flute girl. He enters with the flute girl, followed by a number of the people he has insulted, and continues to insult them in his drunken stupor, but is promptly carried inside by his son. The chorus sing, and soon after Philocleon reappears and performs a wild dance; the chorus, singing and dancing, join him. Then they all leave the stage. The wild dance is in keeping with the earlier revel origins of the *kōmos,* from which Old Comedy sprang.

MIDDLE COMEDY

In the 68 years (404–336 B.C.) between the fall of Athens and the beginning of the Hellenistic age, ushered in by Alexander the Great, King of Macedon (356–323 B.C.), comic poets turned their attention from writing exclusively for Athenians toward writing comedies for the entire Greek world. Consequently, plays and players fanned out from Athens to

Yellow terra-cotta statuettes of Middle Comedy actors, the one with the basket probably bringing some food for a dinner. (Courtesy, The Metropolitan Museum of Art, Rogers Fund [1913].)

supply the vast number of theatres then operating. This new, larger audience was interested in mythological burlesque and plays that mirrored the manners and customs of everyday life. Biting satire and ridicule of public figures were no longer acceptable theatre fare. Comedy now began to replace tragedy as the most vital and vibrant force in fourth-century B.C. theatre. Slaves, courtesans, cooks, parasites, comic old women, procurers, bragging soldiers, young men sowing their wild oats, young men in love, fathers, old bachelors, long-lost daughters—all the later stock characters of New Comedy first appeared in Middle Comedy. The blending of the arts, the chorus as an integral part of the plays, and the *parabasis*—all vital parts of Old Comedy—disappeared. Middle Comedy introduced problems in intrigue, young people in love, seduction, and the discovery of identity by long-lost children.

Today, Middle Comedy is represented by two late comedies of Aristophanes; in both plays, *The Ecclesiazusae* (392/4 B.C.) and *Plutus* (388 B.C.), the *parabasis* is eliminated and the role of the chorus is greatly reduced. There were a vast number of works in this highly productive period which were lost. Names of more than 40 comic poets and the titles of more than 600 plays, along with many short and a few longer fragments, exist. Two of the most prolific comic playwrights were Antiphanes and Alexis of Thurii, who between them wrote well over 500 plays.[15]

NEW COMEDY

The popularity of the plays of Euripides, the newer prevailing philosophical currents in Athens (for Athens was now the established world center for philosophers and teachers), and the new social and economic forces in operation created the background for the flourishing of New Comedy (336–290 B.C.) during the Hellenistic period. Athens was a prosperous city, mildly decadent, and under the domination of the Macedonians. This new age of refinement with its leisured upper and middle classes who had time on their hands to pursue cultural interests furnished the theatre audiences for the New Comedy. The emphasis was on love, romance, marriage, and happy endings.

Audiences enjoyed these aspects of life depicted on the stage by realistic but typical characters in stereotyped plots, repeated over and over again with few variations from one play to another. The most popular situations involved the exposure of children at birth, the stealing of a young child, the seduction and violation of a young girl, and the final recognition of a long-lost daughter by those concerned so that marriage could take place. This continued the trend started with Middle Comedy.

A typical story for a New Comedy "potboiler" went something like this: A young man of good family, whose father is out of town on business, sets out to win the girl he loves. She is enslaved by a procuress who intends to sell her to the highest bidder. A boastful soldier is also competing for the girl. The young man calls upon his intriguing slave and an old bachelor friend of his father's for help. There is much intrigue and confusion. Finally, the young man frees the girl, learns that she is the long-lost daughter of a good family who was stolen in infancy, and a marriage follows.

Menander (ca. 342/1–ca. 293/4 B.C.), Diphilus, Philemon, and many others of the 64 whose names are known furnished Athens and the rest of the Hellenistic world approximately 1,400 New Comedies. The extant remains of their work, aside from that of Menander, consist of fragments varying in length up to about 100 lines.

Of the 108 comedies written by Menander there is one almost complete play, *The Dyskolos*, or *The Man Who Didn't Like People*, a copy of which was found in the Bibliotheca Bodmeriana of Cologny near Geneva in 1957. We also possess half of *The Arbitration*, more than half of *The Shorn Woman* and *The Girl from Samos*, and more than 1,100 fragments from other plays. Menander won eight victories, the first in 315 B.C. His fame was enormous in ancient times, particularly in Rome. He was praised for his realistic style and the skill with which he depicted ordinary citizens.

The ancient Greek plays, whether they were improvisational (mimes and the like) or literary, were created to be performed before an audience. The concern of the next chapter shifts to the theatres built by the Greeks to house their plays.

NOTES

1. A. Andrews, *The Greek Tyrants* (New York: Harper and Row, 1963). Excellent treatment of Greek tyrants.

2. Lillian B. Lawler, *The Dance of the Ancient Greek Theatre* (Iowa City: University of Iowa Press, 1964), p. 6. Very informative and important work on the dances employed in dithyrambs, tragedies, comedies, and satyr plays. See also, by the same author, *The Dance in Ancient Greece* (Middleton, Conn.: Wesleyan University Press, 1964). The definitive work on the monuments pertaining to Greek dance is Germaine Prudhommeau, *La Danse Grècque Antique* (Paris: Editions du Centre National de la Recherche Scientifique, 1965), 2 vols.

3. Gerald F. Else, *The Origin and Early Form of Greek Tragedy* (Cambridge, Mass.: Harvard University Press, 1965), p. 49.

4. Walter F. Otto, *Dionysus: Myth and Cult* (trans. with an introduction by Robert B. Palmer; Bloomington: Indiana University Press, 1965). Contains a very full account of the Dionysus cult. Much material on the dithyramb is to be found in Sir Arthur W. Pickard-Cambridge, *Dithyramb, Tragedy and Comedy* (2nd ed. by T. B. L. Webster; Oxford: Clarendon Press, 1962).

5. *Aristotle's Poetics* (trans. by S. H. Butcher with an introduction by Francis Fergusson; New York: A Dramabook, Hill and Wang, 1961), p. 57 (IV, 12). Excellent edition for students to consult.

6. See Else, *op. cit.,* pp. 1–127. A most stimulating and provocative work. In addition, see his article "The Origin of Tragôidia," *Hermes*, 85 (1957), 17–46. Other works dealing with the origins of tragedy are James Turney Allen, *Stage Antiquities of the Greeks and Romans and their Influence* (New York: Longmans, Green, 1927), pp. 3–16; Margarete Bieber, *The History of the Greek and Roman Theater* (2nd ed. rev. and enlarged; Princeton, N.J.: Princeton University Press, 1961), pp. 1–35; Roy C. Flickinger, *The Greek Theatre and Its Drama* (4th ed.; Chicago: University of Chicago Press, 1936), pp. 1–35; Albin Lesky, *Greek Tragedy* (trans. by H. A. Frankfort with a foreword by E. G. Turner; London: Ernest Benn, 1965), pp. 1–52 especially, remainder of the book is also valuable for a full account of Greek tragedy; and Pickard-Cambridge, *op. cit.,* pp. 60–131.

7. H. D. F. Kitto, "Greek Tragedy and Dionysus," *Theatre Survey*, 1 (1960), 15.

8. See Jane E. Harrison, *Ancient Art and Ritual* (rev. ed.; London: Oxford University Press, 1951), and her other work, *Epilegomena to the Study of Greek Religion, and Themis* (New York: University Books, 1962), pp. 1–577; Herbert J. Muller, *The Spirit of Tragedy* (New York: Knopf, 1956), pp. 3–136; and the two works of William Ridgeway, *The Origin of Tragedy, with Special Reference to the Greek Tragedians* (Cambridge: Cambridge University Press, 1910; reissued by Benjamin Blom, 1965), and *The Dramas and Dramatic Dances of Non-European Races, In Special Reference to the Origin of Greek Tragedy With an Appendix on the Origin of Greek Comedy* (Cambridge: Cambridge University Press, 1915; reissued by Benjamin Blom, 1965).

9. Flickinger, *op. cit.,* p. 23. A succinct account of the birth of satyr drama is presented, pp. 23–25.

10. See the introduction to *Two Satyr Plays* (trans. by Roger Lancelyn Green; Baltimore: Penguin Classics No. 167, 1957), pp. 9–14.

11. *Aristotle's Poetics, op. cit.,* p. 54 (III, 4).

12. See Walter Headlam and A. D. Knox, eds., *Herodas: The Mimes and Fragments, with Notes* (Cambridge: Cambridge University Press, 1922; reissued 1966).

13. See Allardyce Nicoll, *Masks, Mimes and Miracles: Studies in Popular Theatre* (London: George G. Harrap, 1931), pp. 17–50, for a good account of the Doric mimes.

14. See Gilbert Norwood, *Greek Comedy* (London: Methuen, 1931), pp. 114–154, for fragments of the writings of Cratinus and Crates and for an analysis of their work.

15. Katherine Lever, *The Art of Greek Comedy* (London: Methuen, 1956), p. 163. Contains one of the best accounts of Middle Comedy to be found. The sections on Old and New Comedy are also very useful for those interested in the development of Greek comedy. See also Pickard-Cambridge, *op. cit.*

2

GREEK THEATRES

The Greeks were the first people to erect special structures to bring audiences and theatrical performers together. Their theatres (*theatron* a viewing place) built for this purpose helped establish theatre-construction patterns that were followed, with some changes, for centuries. Greek theatres were altered by the Romans to fit their requirements, and new theatres were developed by the Romans which incorporated what they had learned from the Greeks in addition to a few new ideas of their own. These in turn were copied by Italian Renaissance architects when they built their theatres indoors and equipped them with perspective scenery. With modifications the Italian Renaissance theatres furnished the basis for the modern proscenium-arch theatre. In our time Greek theatres have strongly influenced the development of "thrust-stage theatres."

The most reliable first-hand information on ancient Greek theatres is provided by the remains of the theatres themselves. These are found at formerly important, now chiefly deserted, urban centers on the mainland of Greece, on several of the Aegean islands, in Sicily, southern Italy, North Africa, and in the western part of Turkey (Ionia). Their condition varies considerably, depending on the degree of preservation, renovation, or alteration by the Romans and on modern restoration. The Theatre of Epidauros, for example, is now, with the exception of its Hellenistic scene building, in almost perfect working condition. It was protected for centuries by several feet of earth and has recently been carefully restored. At

27

the other extreme are the denuded theatres where just a few scattered stones or fragments of seats are all that is left.

Unfortunately, the present remains of Greek theatres are largely limited to those built during and after the fourth century B.C., and most of these were drastically altered by renovations and conversions in succeeding centuries, particularly by the Romans. Earthquakes, erosion, and pillage have added to the toll. However, the patient, exacting labors of several noted archeologists and theatre scholars whose work spans the last 85 years, have been able to reconstruct, at least on paper, a few of the more important theatres for each period. This has been especially true when their knowledge was fortified by a thorough examination of all monuments pertaining to ancient Greek theatrical productions and included a careful study of the extant Greek plays, to determine how they might have been staged during the fifth and fourth centuries B.C.[1] (Extant Greek plays date from 472 to about 300 B.C.)

CRETAN "THEATRAL AREAS"

The oldest structures which resemble ancient Greek theatres are located on the island of Crete. They date back to the days when the fabulous Minoan civilization flourished. The "theatral area" built about 2000 B.C. at Phaestos, an ancient city located 40 miles southeast of Knossos, contains 10 tiers of stone seats 80 feet long nestled against a palace wall facing a rectangular flagged court, the latter constituting the area where processionals and other activities took place.

The "theatral area" at Knossos (built ca. 1600 B.C.) is located near the northwest corner of the famous palace of Knossos and was so arranged that spectators sat or stood at right angles to each other. On one side there were 18 tiers of stone seats 33 feet long; on the other there were six tiers of stone seats about 50 feet long. These rows of seats met in one corner at a square, raised area which was slightly higher than the top tiers of seats. This was the royal box. The presentation or performance area, bordered on two sides by spectators, was a rectangular space paved with stones, approximately 40 feet by 35 feet, and having a sacred walkway running through the center.

The stone "theatral area" at Phaestos accommodated about 300 spectators, and the one at Knossos about 500. The uses to which these structures were put have never been established; a likely guess is that they were built to house dances, processions, and ceremonial palace functions. Their influence on later Greek theatre design is difficult to establish. They may very likely have been covered over and partially destroyed sometime before the sixth century B.C.

THE EARLIEST ATHENIAN THEATRE

The first theatre built in Greece was located in Athens. A number of authorities place the date for the erection of the earliest Theatre of Dionysus around 534 B.C., concurrent with the official start of tragedy. Some place it even earlier, about 550 B.C. The exact location of this theatre is also in dispute. One theory holds that the theatre was located in the agora, the ancient marketplace below the Acropolis. All that was required for these early performances was an open space for the performers, a *thymele* (an altar or sacrificial table), and temporary wooden *ikria* (bleachers) rising in tiers one above the other for seating the audience. It is reported in Suidas that the bleachers collapsed and several people were killed during a contest in 499 B.C. among the dramatists Aeschylus, Pratinas, and Choerilus.

The following year the contest was moved to a sacred precinct on the south side of the Acropolis. An area dedicated to Dionysus Eleuthereus was established around the middle of the sixth century B.C.; it contained a temple with a *thymele* in front of it and an orchestra (dancing place) to accommodate early Dionysian ceremonies.

Another possibility suggested is that the first Athenian theatre was located from the beginning in the precinct of Dionysus Eleuthereus and that it was there that the bleachers collapsed rather than in the agora.

CLASSICAL THEATRES[2]

The Theatre of Dionysus which came into being in Athens in the fifth century B.C. following the bleacher incident assumed a position of tremendous importance. In this theatre the plays of Aeschylus, Sophocles, Euripides, Aristophanes, and the other prominent dramatists of the period were first performed. Moreover, this theatre was in use for centuries, changing its form and architectural details to conform to later developments.

Besides the Theatre of Dionysus, the other classical theatre which will be considered here is the Theatre of Epidauros. However, before a detailed description of these theatres, something needs to be said about the general structural characteristics of classical Greek theatres. They eventu-

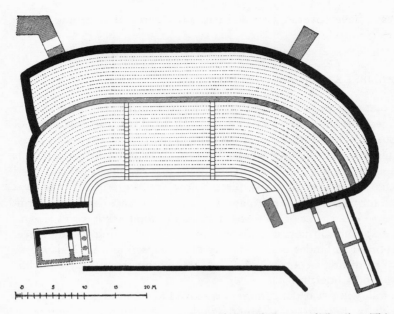

Ground plan of Theatre of Thorikos. This theatre was never equipped with a permanent scene building. (From Dörpfeld and Reisch, *Griechische Theater* [1896].)

ally, with few exceptions, consisted of three distinct parts: *theatron* (viewing place) for spectators; orchestra (dancing place), where chorus and actors performed; and a later addition, a *skene* (scene building), which provided a scenic backing. The theatres were normally located near a populated area at the bottom of or cut out of a carefully selected, sloping hillside overlooking a seascape, a plain, or a city. If the chosen hillside consisted of suitable material (limestone), the theatre benches were simply carved out of it. This was true for the theatres at Argos (fourth century B.C.), Syracuse (fifth century B.C.), and Chaeronea (fourth century B.C.). The most common method was to bring in native stone for the seats. The circular orchestra located adjacent to and almost completely surrounded on three sides by the *theatron* was approximately 65 feet in diameter. On either side of the extremities of the *theatron* bordering the orchestra was open space for the *parodoi* (lateral entrances into the orchestra) used by chorus members for initial entrances into the playing area, by the actors suggesting in their stage appearance arrival from the harbor or distant parts, and by the audience to reach the lower sections of seats. In many theatres the *parodoi* developed subsequently into imposing stone gateways, like the ones at the Theatre of Epidauros. They helped to unify the separate parts of the theatre: *orchestra, skene,* and *theatron*. A *thymele* (altar) was usually located in the middle of the orchestra; however, it could be placed to one side of the orchestra, as it was in the Theatre of Thorikos and in the later Hellenistic Theatre of Priene.

The earliest scene buildings were very simple wooden structures. Later they were converted into increasingly complex stone buildings with *paraskenia* (side wings), several doors, a columned *proskenion* (section in front of the *skene*), an additional story, as well as other features. The development of the scene buildings into more complex structures paralleled the increased interest in acting, scenery, New Comedies rather than tragedies, and the diminished use of the chorus.) In the Hellenistic theatres, the scene buildings with their raised stages dominated.

THEATRE OF DIONYSUS

The Theatre of Dionysus (ca. 499/8–ca. 150 B.C.) underwent at least four fundamental changes during the classical period and was not converted into a Hellenistic theatre until quite late, nearly 200 years after the latter made its appearance.

Reconstruction of Theatre of Dionysus and temple (ca. 480 B.C.). (Drawing by Martha Kaufman.)

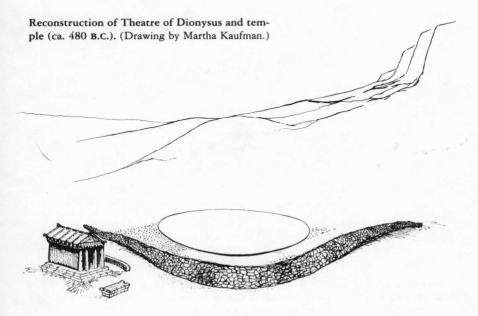

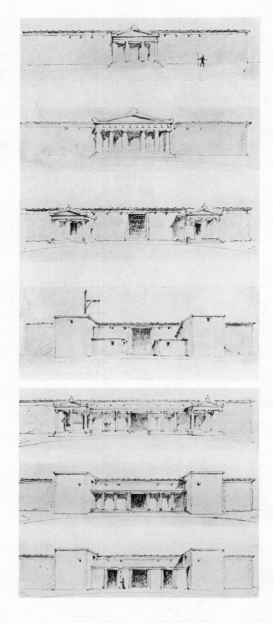

Reconstructions of possible scene buildings in Theatre of Dionysus during second half of 5th cent. **B.C.** (From Fiechter, *Antike Griechische Theaterbauten: Dionysostheater III* [1936]. Courtesy, Verlag W. Kohlhammer Gmbh, Stuttgart.)

In the early part of the fifth century B.C., this theatre consisted of a circular orchestra area some 85 feet in diameter, cut out of the hillside, leveled, and hard-packed. It was supported on one side by a curved retaining wall, and in the center of the orchestra a *thymele* was placed.[3] The theatre was located between the sloping south side of the Acropolis and the small Temple of Dionysus in the precinct of Dionysus Eleuthereus. The *theatron* was the hillside, subsequently provided with wooden planks covering the earthen tiers dug out of the hillside. Presumably, there was no scene building. In this theatre were staged the earliest fifth-century Athenian dithyrambs, tragedies, Old Comedies, and satyr plays.

Exactly when the scene building first appeared in the Theatre of Dionysus is a question of uncertain answer. The first literary evidence of a scene building is found in *The Oresteia* of Aeschylus, produced in 458 B.C. One recent authority even dates the existence of some kind of a scene building in the earliest period.[4] The early scene buildings were evidently quite crude, temporary wooden structures erected for each festival near the edge of the orchestra area and probably, because they occupied a portion of it, the orchestra was reduced in diameter from 85 to 65 feet.[5] The scene buildings could serve as scenic backing for plays when needed and could also be used as dressing rooms for the actors.

When Pericles built his odeion (a roofed concert hall) in 446–442 B.C., immediately east of the Theatre of Dionysus, it encroached on the theatre. It thus became necessary to shift the orchestra and *theatron* a few feet to the northwest, thereby making the *theatron* steeper. The old curved retaining wall built to support the south side of the orchestra was replaced by a long straight wall consisting of large breccia blocks.[6] Between this wall and the older Temple of Dionysus a long wooden hall, or stoa, about 200 feet long and 20 feet wide was constructed. The floor of the stoa was approximately 8 feet below the orchestra level, which was reached by a double flight of interior stairs. At the top of the stairs was a large opening in the north wall of the stoa about 23 feet wide leading out onto the orchestra terrace and onto a "T foundation" (see the figure on p. 34) made of blocks of stone and flush with the orchestra level. It jutted out from the stoa opening about 10 feet and was about 25 feet wide. On either side of the "T foundation" located in the new retaining wall and independent of the stoa were 10 vertical stone grooves or slots which could be used to support temporary wooden scene buildings.

The extensive changes made at the Theatre of Dionysus during the reign of Pericles also included the construction of a new, larger Temple of Dionysus south of the older one. Pickard-Cambridge gave this renovated Theatre of Dionysus the subtitle of "Periclean Theatre."

It is thought that the wooden stoa was replaced by one made of stone about 421–415 B.C.

The last major renovation of the Theatre of Dionysus in the classical period occurred during the term of the orator Lycurgus, who was in charge of Athenian finances from 338 to 326 B.C. This "Lycurgean Theatre" lasted until about 150 B.C., at which time it was converted into a Hellenistic theatre.

Lycurgus installed 78 rows of stone seats. These rested on a natural rock foundation and built-up earth. Divided into three sections separated by two passageways (diazomata), they seated from 14,000 to 17,000 people. The 67 special chair seats or thrones, each bearing the name of the priest or high official for whom it was reserved, were arranged in the first row facing the orchestra. Of these, 60 are still extant (dating perhaps from a later period). A special decorative throne, with holes near the feet for holding a supporting canopy for the priest of Dionysus, was located in the center of the row of chairs.

Between the orchestra and the stone stoa a new permanent stone *skene* was constructed with two projecting side wings (paraskenia) one or two stories high. This *skene* undoubtedly underwent several changes during the many years of its use. Perhaps stone columns were placed in front of it, or sections of it, such as the *paraskenia,* thereby creating a decorative

Ground plan of section of Theatre of Dionysus showing position of old orchestra (ca. 458 B.C.) and new orchestra (ca. 442 B.C.). The old, partially circular retaining wall and the new retaining wall with its 10 stone slots and "T foundation" are also shown. (Drawing by Martha Kaufman.)

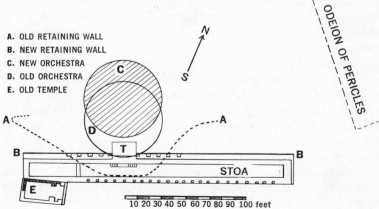

A. OLD RETAINING WALL
B. NEW RETAINING WALL
C. NEW ORCHESTRA
D. OLD ORCHESTRA
E. OLD TEMPLE

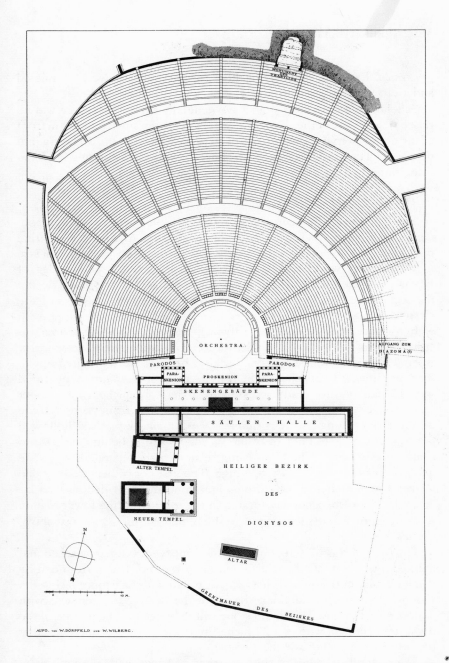

Ground plan of precinct of Dionysus Eleuthereus after Lycurgus converted Theatre of Dionysus into a stone theatre (ca. 338–326 B.C.). (From Dörpfeld and Reisch, _Griechische Theater_ [1896].)

proskenion. Excellent drainage facilities for the orchestra were completed and were much as they are today.

Scholars in the past few years have generally agreed that there was no raised stage in any of the classical theatres aside from small porches in front of the entrance to the *skene* or sets of steps leading from the orchestra into the *skene*.[7] The raised stage was introduced into theatre building in Hellenistic times.

THEATRE OF EPIDAUROS

The Theatre of Epidauros (ca. 350 B.C.) is located in the Peloponnesus, approximately 110 miles by highway from Athens at the shrine of Asclepius, a famous healing center. It was the most beautiful theatre in the ancient world and was often referred to as "the wonder of Epidauros." Designed by Polyclitus the Younger, it was built during the second half of the fourth century B.C., in the waning years of the classical period.

In order to construct it, a perfectly proportioned, semicircular area was carved out of the side of Mt. Chynortion to accommodate the *theatron.* Then 55 rows of white-limestone backless benches were installed in two sections: 34 tiers of benches in the lower section of the *theatron,* provided with 13 stairways for ready access; and 21 tiers of benches in the upper section, steeper and provided with 23 stairways. The front portion of the benches, the seating part, was slightly raised; the back part was hollowed out to accommodate the feet of the spectators sitting behind and also to drain off rain water. The two seating sections were separated by a wide *diazoma* skirted by a wall 4½ feet high. The first tier of benches, the one nearest to the orchestra, was of pink limestone and provided with backs. A similar tier of benches was located in the top row of the lower seating section, another in the lowest row of the upper seating section just above the *diazoma.*

The orchestra is 62½ feet in diameter, unpaved, but hard-packed and marked by a complete, circular limestone threshold. It is surrounded by a half-circular curbstone, 16 feet across, paved with flagstones facing the *theatron.* It serves as a drainage basin for the theatre and connects with underground drains. The round stone still to be seen in the middle of the orchestra and level with it is 28 inches in diameter. It probably served at one time as an anchor for the *thymele.*

The over-all diameter of this theatre is 387 feet, with the top tier of benches 74 feet above the orchestra level. It seats 14,000 spectators. Its acoustics are perfect: a mere whisper in the orchestra is easily heard in the farthest seats.

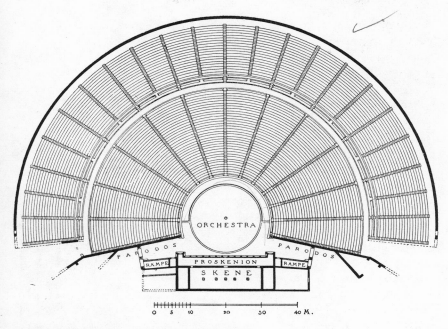

Ground plan of Theatre of Epidauros during Hellenistic period. (From Dörpfeld and Reisch, *Griechische Theater* [1896].)

The theatre of Epidauros is the best-preserved and finest example of a classical theatre that we have in the world today. The only part altered in any way from its original form is the *skene,* in spite of much restorative work to repair earthquake damage. When the theatre was first built, the *skene* was a temporary wooden building which served merely as a backing for the dramatic action depicted in the orchestra. During the later Hellenistic period, in keeping with the newer theatre-building trend and the increased emphasis on acting, a stone *skene* was installed with a raised stage 11½ feet high, 8 feet deep, and 85 feet wide. The stage wall was pierced by three large openings *(thyromata)*. The stage level was reached on either side by sloping ramps ascending from the foot of the stone *parodoi* (lateral entranceways flanking the theatre between the *skene* and *theatron*). These large limestone double *parodoi* leading into each side of the lower section of the theatre have recently been restored. They are 21 feet high and rest against the northeastern and northwestern *analemma* (lateral sustaining walls) of the theatre. The upper section of the theatre is reached by sloping earthen ramps leading to the *diazoma*.[8]

the
one
of
these
3

Three views of ruins of Theatre of Epidauros. (Courtesy, Nick Stournaras.)

HELLENISTIC THEATRES[9]

During the fourth, third, and second centuries B.C., basic alterations were made in theatre architecture which resulted in what has been termed the Hellenistic theatre. Most of the changes were made in the *skene* section of the theatre. It was moved forward in some theatres into the orchestra area, reducing it to a semicircle, or in some instances to an elongated semicircle. The front portion of the *skene* was converted into a *proskenion–logeion,* a high, raised stage varying in height from about 8 to 12 feet, in width from about 45 to 140 feet, and in depth from about 6½ to 14 feet. The back wall of this high stage was provided with doors, usually from one to three, that opened onto it. Later the doors were replaced by a series of *thyromata* (large openings). They varied in number in the different theatres from one to seven. The stage was supported in front by a series of open columns, and between them *pinakes* (removable painted screens) could be inserted to provide changeable scenic backing. *Periaktoi* (triangu-

Reconstruction of section of Hellenistic Theatre of Oropus showing open *thyromata* and ramp leading onto the high stage. (From Fiechter, *Antike Griechische Theaterbauten: Das Theater in Oropus I* [1930]. Courtesy, Verlag W. Kohlhammer Gmbh, Stuttgart.)

lar wooden prisms with a different scene painted on each side) came into use sometime during the Hellenistic period and were probably located near the side entrances of the stage. *Periaktoi* and *pinakes* made it possible to achieve more realistic stage settings capable of being changed relatively quickly.

New theatres constructed after 336 B.C., as well as many of those already built, were affected by the emerging Hellenistic pattern that lasted approximately 300 years, to the Roman conquest of the Grecian world. It became the dominant style for nearly all operating theatres during this period. Older theatres were converted and new ones adopted it.

In the fourth century B.C., acting gained in importance as the quality of playwriting declined from the previous century's high level. Contests among actors at festivals attracted more attention than did those among playwrights. The birth of theatrical guilds in the third century B.C. helped all theatre artists, especially actors, gain greater status and public adulation. The actors became increasingly interested in theatres that would better display their talents. A high platform stage naturally provided a better vantage point from which to perform.

Euripidean tragedy, with its skepticism and retreat from the heroic qualities of an earlier period, influenced the later Hellenistic tragedy. It has been suggested that the raised stage, the *onkos* (the extended hairpiece of the tragic actor's mask), and the *kothornos* (elevated shoe worn by tragic actors) were Hellenistic devices intended physically to return some of the lost stature to tragic heroes.[10] In this way, tragic heroes were decidedly separated from the ordinary men who formed the chorus.

The once-popular tragedy, however, lost most of its audience to the New Comedy, with its emphasis on individual characters, intriguing action, and realism. Choral songs were no longer composed for individual comedies and could readily be "transferred from play to play."[11] The choruses for Menander's plays are mere commentaries between the episodes and have no connection with the plots.

The development of the New Comedies paralleled the development of the new raised Hellenistic theatre stages.[12] As New Comedies, with their great popular appeal, began to appear, efforts to produce them as effectively as possible must surely have been made. The high, raised stages would have brought the actors into greater prominence and provided excellent playing areas. The stage became the street, and the back wall with its doors represented the two or three houses which were needed. This type of stage setting is clearly indicated by some of the surviving portions of Menander's plays as well as the extant plays of Plautus and

Terence which were Roman translations and adaptations of Greek originals.

THEATRE OF PRIENE

The Hellenistic theatre pattern did not originate at Priene, but it did evolve there from a fairly early date. Priene was an Ionian city located on the western coast of Turkey, a few miles south of Ephesus. It was completely refounded on a new site in the middle of the fourth century B.C. and was laid out according to a preconceived or "master plan" which included the theatre. Alexander the Great found the city under construction when he passed through it in 334 B.C. and agreed to pay for the Temple of Athena in return for the privilege of dedicating it, which he did when it was completed.[13] It was most fitting that this particular city should have fostered a new type of theatre.

The Theatre of Priene (ca. 330 B.C.) is a good starting point for investigating Hellenistic theatres. Its scene building is well preserved and relatively free of later Roman changes. A reasonably accurate reconstruction of it is possible because the Romans failed to obliterate or alter its basic shape. Painstaking research carried out on this theatre by Armin von Gerkan in 1911–1912, has produced a tremendous amount of information.[14] This research, combined with material drawn from other sources, yields most of the general characteristics common to all Hellenistic theatres.

Construction on this theatre began about 334 B.C., concurrent with the rebuilding of the city of Priene. The first completed sections, about 330 B.C., were the unpaved orchestra, approximately 50 feet in diameter, and the stone (Mykale marble), semielliptical *theatron,* which seated approximately 6,000. A *diazoma* separated the *theatron* into two sections: 25 tiers of seats in the upper section, and 22 tiers of seats in the lower. All that remains of these seats today are supports for nine rows bordering the passageway between them and the *proedria* (front row of seats next to the orchestra). The *proedria* for seating dignitaries, evidently not in the original plan, was added later, in the third century B.C., and occupied an area immediately surrounding the orchestra. It contained a row of stone benches with backs and five decorative stone throne chairs with built-in footstools. They were inserted into the row of benches at five random spots. A sacrificial altar for burnt offerings was installed about 200 B.C. in the middle of the *proedria* rather than in the center of the orchestra.

It is conceivable that for several years this theatre used a temporary

View of ruins of Theatre of Priene. (From Gerkan, *Das Theater von Priene* [Munich: Benjamin Harz Verlag, 1921]. Courtesy, Ester Sass and M. Harz.)

wooden *skene* similar to those in classical theatres. When a stone scene building was finally built toward the end of the third century or later in the second century B.C., it was a rectangular two-story structure about 60 feet long, 19 feet wide, and 15 feet high. The lower story, used for prop storage and dressing areas, was divided into three rooms nearly equal in size. Door openings led from each of the rooms into the orchestra.

Fronting this building and facing the orchestra was a *proskenion-logeion,* a single-story porchlike appendage about 65 feet long, 9½ feet wide, and 9 feet high which reduced the orchestra from its circular form to an elongated semicircle. It was supported by a series of 12 columns, 10 with Doric half-columns attached on the front sides. The roof *(logeion)* of this "porch" was flat, covered with heavy wooden planking, and used as a stage. One large double door opened from the second-story level onto it; later two more were added. Sometime in the second century B.C. the doors were replaced by *thyromata,* in which set pieces, furnishing, curtains, and decorations could be placed. When needed, large double doors could be inserted into the openings. Depending on the productions, some might have been closed off by curtains or *pinakes* (painted wooden panels). At

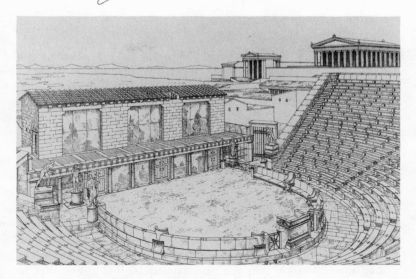

Reconstruction of Theatre of Priene during 2nd cent. B.C. (From Gerkan, *Das Theater von Priene* [Munich: Benjamin Harz Verlag, 1921]. Courtesy, Ester Sass and M. Harz.)

one end of the stage, steps led up to the *logeion* from the rear of the building.

At either end of the scene building, but not facing the orchestra, a small door opened onto the end sections of the stage—the "wings"—used by actors for making entrances. The spaces between the columns supporting the stage were filled in three ways: the end spaces were closed off by delicate grillwork; some of the remaining spaces were taken up with three wooden double doors equidistant from each other, opening onto the orchestra; while the spaces still left were filled with *pinakes* fastened into place between the columns by means of sockets cut into the supporting stone columns. Similar sockets in supporting stage columns are to be found at the Theatre of Oropus and other Hellenistic theatres.

After the stone *skene* was built in the Theatre of Priene, additional seats of honor were installed in the *theatron* at a higher level behind and above the altar. The new high stage made improved sight lines necessary.

The two marble *parodoi*, located between the *skene* and the *analemma* (supporting walls of the *theatron*), somewhat smaller but otherwise resembling those at the Theatre of Epidauros, were fitted with iron gates closing off gateways into the theatre when it was not in use.

OTHER IMPORTANT THEATRES

Moderately well-preserved and significant Hellenistic theatres, aside from the one at Priene, are those at Oropus, Delos, Ephesus, and Pergamum. Other important theatres constructed originally as Hellenistic or classical but later converted were at Assus, Athens (Theatre of Dionysus), Argos, Corinth, Delphi, Dodona, Epidauros, Eretria, Magnesia, Megalopolis, Miletus, New Pleuron, Oeniadae, Perge, Piraeus, Pompeii (large theatre), Segesta, Sicyon, Sparta, Sycracuse, Taormina, Thasos, Tyndaris, and Zea.

Of this group the Theatre of Pergamum in western Turkey, built sometime between 197 and 159 B.C., merits special attention. From the top row of seats to the orchestra 82 rows below, the *theatron* extends a distance of 175 feet, making it the steepest Greek theatre. The rows of seats are fan-shaped, thus differing considerably from the more common slightly elongated and semicircular *theatron*. The seats, separated into three sections by two *diazomata,* accommodated 16,000 spectators, who looked almost straight down on an orchestra 69 feet in diameter reduced to a half-circle by a narrow terrace. This terrace served as a connecting

Reconstruction of scene building and orchestra of Hellenistic theatre at Delos. Many authorities believe there were three *thyromata,* rather than one as shown here. (From Dörpfeld and Reisch, *Griechische Theater* [1896].)

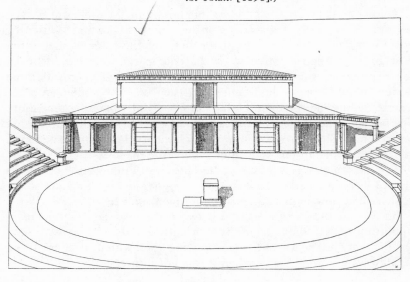

passageway from the agora to the Temple of Dionysus, located near the theatre. During theatrical performances a portable wooden Hellenistic-type scene building was set up on this terrace. Its supports were anchored in three rows of hard stone provided with slots about 14 inches square sunken in the ground; 42 of these slotted stones, many in their original positions, may still be found among the terrace ruins. These stone slots and the use to which they were put help to explain the probable function of the stone slots contained in the new retaining wall of the Theatre of Dionysus after about 442 B.C., when they were used to support scene buildings.

The Hellenistic *skene,* so popular outside of Athens and particularly in Asia Minor, finally reached the Theatre of Dionysus in the second century B.C. Its scene building was then converted and provided with a high, raised stage.

POSSIBLE ORIGINS OF THE SKENE

A puzzling and pervasive problem in tracing the development of new theatrical staging methods, most particularly the stage itself, has to do with determining the origins. We have seen that the Hellenistic *skene* was basically an elongated, two-story rectangular building with varying numbers of large openings *(thyromata)* at the second-story level directly opening onto the *proskenion-logeion,* a flat-roofed portico supported by an open colonnade facing the orchestra. While the entire structure could be made of wood, it was built most often of stone in the second and first centuries B.C. Ultimately, it was "an adaptation of a one-storeyed flat-roofed type of portico which sometimes was provided along the exterior of a large two-storeyed building, in order to give direct access from the stairs to every portion of the upper floor."[15]

Fortunately, the architectural progenitors for this type of theatre have been admirably investigated by Margarete Bieber. She has found its ancestors in several temples in Asia Minor, in ancient Egypt's "so called soul houses dating from the Eleventh and Twelfth Dynasties," in the Leonidaion hostel of the fourth century B.C. at Olympia, and in the Villa of Mysteries at Pompeii.[16]

HELLENISTIC THEATRES IN RETROSPECT

Hellenistic theatres ranged in size from the small, intimate Theatre of Oropus (30 miles north of Athens at the Sanctuary of Amphiaros) seating 3,000 and the Theatre of Priene seating 6,000 to the huge Theatre of

Argos seating 20,000, of Megalopolis (largest theatre in antiquity on the mainland of Greece and located in the heart of the Peloponnesus, 22 miles southwest of Tripolis) seating 21,000, and of Ephesus (located in western Turkey) seating 25,000. There were many theatres in the middle range seating from 6,000 to 19,000.

The height, depth, and width of the stages in these theatres also varied considerably. For example, the Theatre of Oropus had a stage that was 8 feet high, 6½ feet deep, and 44¾ feet wide; the stage at the Theatre of Priene was 9 feet high, 9½ feet deep, and 65 feet wide; the stage at the Theatre of Epidauros was 11½ feet high, 8 feet deep, and 85 feet wide, and the Theatre of Ephesus was 8½ feet high, 14 feet deep, and 137 feet wide.

The number of *thyromata* found in Hellenistic theatres also varied greatly: there was one in the Theatre of Delos; one and later three in the Theatre of Priene; three in the Theatre of Eretria, Pergamum, Corinth, New Pleuron, Epidauros; five in the Theatre of Oropus, Sicyon, Oeniadae; and seven in the Theatre of Ephesus and Miletus.

Sloping ramps leading up to the stage on each side were used in the Theatre of Oropus, Epidauros, Sicyon, Corinth, and Eretria. The last-named used ramps which, because of the conformation of the ground surrounding the *skene,* did not slant. Steps instead of ramps were used at the Theatre of Priene.

Special openings in the roofs of scene buildings at Priene and Corinth, and perhaps also in other Hellenistic theatres as well, were provided for the appearance of gods.[17]

There is no agreement among theatre scholars concerning how Hellenistic theatres were utilized in staging plays.[18] Nevertheless, it seems most reasonable to assume that they approximated the concept of today's "flexible theatre," at once accommodating the "new" Hellenistic drama as well as revivals of "old" classical plays. The high stage and its *thyromata* easily plugged with wooden doors to represent house fronts made ideal, extremely workable stage settings for most New Comedies. When necessary, some scenes could easily have been played in and spilled out of the *thyromata.* The limited chorus characteristic of early New Comedy could have performed on such stages without difficulty. In later years, judging from extant Roman comedies of this genre, the chorus was dispensed with entirely.

Revivals of older tragedies, with their large choruses, could still be effectively staged in the lower parts of the theatres, at the orchestra level. Facilities for staging such plays remained. They were relatively unaltered, except that the orchestra areas in many theatres had been reduced in size

Production of Euripides' *Heracleidae* by Greek National Theatre in Theatre of Epidauros during Festival of Epidauros in 1970. (Courtesy, Greek State Theatre Organisation.)

Production of Sophocles' *The Women of Trachis* by Greek National Theatre in Theatre of Epidauros during Festival of Epidauros in 1970. (Courtesy, Greek State Theatre Organisation.)

and in several others made semicircular. Yet more than adequate room was retained for chorus performance. Where needed, doors could be inserted in the colonnaded front wall and remaining spaces filled with *pinakes,* thus providing productions with scenic decor.

If necessary, these theatres would lend themselves to the combined use of the high stage and the orchestra. Such combinations would have been most appropriate for those later tragedies in which the chorus did not dance actively nor participate in the action, but merely sang or recited choral odes as interludes. The chorus may well have reached this state of development in tragedies written during the second century B.C.

CURRENT USE OF ANCIENT THEATRES

During the last few summers the Greek National Theatre, with the aid of the Greek government, has been presenting ancient Greek plays (in modern Greek adaptations) in several of the partially restored theatres. These include the Theatre of Epidauros and of Herodes Atticus, and more recently the Theatre of Dodona and of Delphi. More activity of this kind is planned for the future. The handling of the chorus, the staging, and the acting style used in these productions help immensely toward a better understanding and appreciation of the plays of Aeschylus, Sophocles, Euripides, and Aristophanes. The methods whereby these plays might have been produced, staged, and acted when first given—the production processes of the Greek theatre of antiquity—form the subject of the next chapter.

NOTES

1. Some of the outstanding theatre scholars whose works are in English and should be consulted on this matter are James Turney Allen, "The Key to the Reconstruction of the Fifth-Century Theater at Athens," *University of California Publications in Philology,* 5 (1918), 55–58, and "The Greek Theater of the Fifth Century before Christ," *University of California Publications in Philology,* 7 (1919), 1–119; Margarete Bieber, *The History of the Greek and Roman Theater* (2nd ed. rev. and enlarged; Princeton, N.J.: Princeton University Press, 1961); Roy C. Flickinger, *The Greek Theatre and Its Drama* (6th ed. enlarged; Chicago: University of Chicago Press, 1960); Sir Arthur W. Pickard-Cambridge, *The Theatre of Dionysus in Athens* (Oxford: Clarendon Press, 1946); and T. B. L. Webster, *Greek Theatre Production* (London: Methuen, 1956; 2nd ed., 1970).
2. The classical period included the fifth and fourth centuries to 336 B.C.
3. Carlo Anti believes that the early orchestra for the Theatre of Dionysus may

have been almost square in shape. See his work, *Teatri Greci Arcaici da Minosse a Pericle* (Padua, 1947).

4. Peter D. Arnott, *Greek Scenic Conventions in the Fifth Century B.C.* (Oxford: Clarendon Press, 1962), pp. 4–6.

5. Bieber, *op. cit.*, p. 57.

6. Pickard-Cambridge, *op. cit.*, p. 16.

7. Arnott, *op. cit.*, p. 18, contends that the Greek theatres of the classical period had a stage about 4 feet high connected by a flight of steps to the ground-level orchestra area.

8. Detailed information on the Theatre of Epidauros is contained in Armin von Gerkan and Wolfgang Müller-Wiener, *Das Theater von Epidauros* (Stuttgart: W. Kohlhammer, 1961).

9. The Hellenistic period extended from 336 B.C., when Alexander the Great became King of Macedonia, to the Battle of Actium in 31 B.C.

10. G. M. Sifakis, *Studies in the History of Hellenistic Drama* (London: University of London, Athlone Press, 1967), pp. 133–134. Sifakis deals with the history of dramatic performances in Delos and Delphi. Appendices I and II are very important.

11. *Ibid.*, p. 113.

12. William Bell Dinsmoor, *The Architecture of Ancient Greece: An Account of Its Historic Development* (3rd ed. rev.; London: B. T. Batsford, 1950), pp. 298–299.

13. George E. Bean, *Aegean Turkey: An Archaeological Guide* (London: Ernest Benn, 1966), pp. 198–199. This book and J. M. Cook, *The Greeks in Ionia and the East* (London: Ernest Benn, 1962), contain much material on Greek and Roman ruins in Turkey.

14. See Armin von Gerkan, *Das Theater von Priene* (Munich, 1921). Most of the information on the Theatre of Priene presented in this chapter is based on this work.

15. A. W. Lawrence, *Greek Architecture* (Baltimore: Penguin Books, 1957), p. 286.

16. Bieber, *op. cit.*, p. 112.

17. Sifakis, *op. cit.*, p. 129.

18. Summaries of theories put forth by scholars on the probable staging used in Hellenistic theatres can be found in Bieber, *op. cit.*, pp. 114–116, and Sifakis, *op. cit.*, pp. 126–135.

3

THEATRICAL PRODUCTION IN GREECE

Athens was the center, the theatrical hub, of the entire Hellenic world. The atmosphere there was conducive to theatre which developed, thrived, and led a vigorous life after it was introduced and remained thus for centuries. New plays were written each year, and playwrights competed for the honor of having their works produced in contests that were the most important part of civic festivals—public ceremonies, open to everybody. Competitions for prizes and recognition were deeply embodied in many phases of Greek life. Poets read their lyrics, rhapsodists delivered ancient epics, flutists played their latest compositions, and choruses performed the newest dithyrambs—all competed in contests.

THEATRE FESTIVALS

Theatrical productions in Athens were confined to two great yearly festivals: the Lenaea and the Great Dionysia, or City Dionysia. A third festival, the Rural Dionysia, which was held each year in the larger Attic districts, eventually included plays along with its other activities.[1]

Dionysian festivals, with their competitive dramatic performances and performers, gained even greater popularity in the Hellenistic age and were held in all parts of the Greek world. Sometimes, these contests were incorporated into other festivals.[2]

RURAL DIONYSIA

Each year, toward the end of December and the beginning of January, Rural Dionysia were celebrated in several villages in Attica. In their early years, probably in the sixth and fifth centuries, they featured a phallic procession to encourage crop fertility for the coming spring. Sacrifices were offered and competitions in songs and dances were held, as were matches to see who could stand the longest on a filled, oiled wineskin. Even though the festival had nothing directly to do with wine, the latter was drunk in great quantities. By tradition, the program of activities was different in each deme (district).

Most of the information concerning the Rural Dionysia comes from the fourth century B.C. By this time, traveling companies of players were performing comedies and tragedies which had already been given in Athens. They visited such centers as Eleusis, Icaria, Salamis, Rhamnus, Thorikus, and Piraeus. The Piraeus Dionysian festival, one of the largest in Greece, was crowded with people from Athens and elsewhere. Dithyrambic contests were included with the plays, the choruses drawn from members of visiting companies and supplemented by local participants.

Rural Dionysia were scheduled at different times in the districts, enabling traveling companies to visit several places during a single tour. Extensive touring eventually stimulated and focused attention on performers and helped to give rise to the formation of guilds, such as "The Artists of Dionysus," to protect and further the interests of poets as well as all types of performing artists.

LENAEA

The festival of the Lenaea, so important for the development of comedy, was held in the last days of January and in early February in a sacred grove called the Lenaeum located just west of the Acropolis. The festival's name stems from *lenai* (maenads, or mad women) and their initiation into the Dionysian mysteries. Older than the City Dionysia, it came to Athens from the north, near the beginning of the sixth century B.C., perhaps by way of ancient Thebes. The earliest festivals were given over to a procession of wandering revelers, to sacrifices, and to initiation rites. Sometime between 580 and 560 B.C. informal performances of *kōmoi* (revels) were held and Old Comedy began to take form. Records of what occurred to comedy during its developmental period between 560 and 432 B.C. have not been preserved. Comedy contests may have been organized at the Lenaea before those at the City Dionysia, but not formally recognized. The first official production of a comedy in Athens took place at the City Dionysia in 487/6 B.C.

There has been scholarly speculation concerning a Lenaean theatre once thought to have been located in the Sanctuary of Dionysus, a marshy hollow between the west slope of the Acropolis, the Aeropagus, and the Pnyx; or it may have been located in the agora. Information on this theatre is very fragmentary. Some plays must have been given there. However, when tragedy contests were introduced at the Lenaea festival about 422 B.C., between two tragic playwrights competing, each with two tragedies, it is thought that the contest was moved to the Theatre of Dionysus and that a contest for tragic actors was begun at the same time. Ten years later, in 432 B.C., contests among five comic playwrights, each represented by one play, and contests for comic actors were introduced. For a short period of time during the Peloponnesian War, competing comic poets were reduced to three. In some form, Lenaean festival contests lasted down to about the first century B.C.

One of this festival's great advantages was that it occurred in winter, which meant smaller crowds and an audience likely to be free of foreigners. The comic playwrights could therefore be freer in handling controversial issues and personages. This feature is attested by this line from *The Acharnians* of Aristophanes: "Cleon shall not be able to accuse me of attacking Athens before strangers; we are by ourselves at the festival of the Lenaea." Younger playwrights were given opportunities to try out their works at the Lenaea. Comic playwrights, because they furnished only one play for each festival, could easily enter plays for the Lenaea and the City Dionysia in the same year.

CITY DIONYSIA

The famous City Dionysia, last of the great festivals introduced in Athens, was established about 534 B.C. by the tyrant Pisistratus, a man who rose to the aristocratic clans of Athens, to celebrate the popular god Dionysus. It was in honor of Dionysus Eleuthereus and given yearly in the latter part of March and in early April. This particular Dionysian cult came from the small Attic village of Eleutherae, located 34 miles northwest of Athens. When introduced into Athens, the cult brought with it a wooden statue of the god, which was placed in a small temple erected for it just below the Acropolis, on the southwest side. On festival days the statue was removed from the temple and placed on an altar nearby to "observe" the ceremonies. The area around the temple became a sacred sanctuary, later the site for the Theatre of Dionysus.

Held annually until about 120 B.C., the festival varied greatly during this time span of more than 400 years, with respect to the procedures followed, the activities included, the number and variety of plays given, and the actual length.

Ceremonies held preceding and following the City Dionysia were usually crowded into two days. The day prior to opening was allotted to a proagon (precontest) followed by a religious procession. The proagon was a preview heralding the forthcoming festival plays. It was introduced in 444 B.C. and held in the newly completed odeion of Pericles. Playwrights announced the subjects of their plays; *choregoi* (producers), actors, chorus members, and flute players were presented to the audience. Later in the day, thousands of celebrants participated in a huge, colorful procession. The statue of Dionysus Eleuthereus was taken out of his temple and carried to the Academy, a sacred grove two miles west of Athens, on the road to Eleutherae. Sacrifices were offered, rites performed, and as night fell a torchlight procession brought the statue back to the theatre, where it was placed on an altar to watch over and enjoy the forthcoming ceremonies and contests. The processional was a reenactment of a part of the original journey which brought the statue of Dionysus to Athens.

A day or two after the festival proper, the *ekklēsia* (Athenian assembly) met for the purpose of examining the conduct of festival officials. Also, persons who had been caught violating the peace or committing other transgressions during the festival were tried and severely punished.

The first and second days of the festival during the fifth century B.C. were given over to the staging of two dithyramb contests. The first one involved 10 choruses of boys, and the second 10 choruses of men. There were 50 members in each chorus making a total of 1,000 participants dancing and singing. They were accompanied by 20 flute players, one per chorus. Each of the 10 Attic tribes was responsible for furnishing two choruses, a men's and a boys'. The long day's festivities closed each evening with processional revels.

After 487/6 B.C. the third day was given over to five comic playwrights, each competing with a single play. The fourth, fifth, and sixth days were devoted to competitions among tragic playwrights, each of whom furnished a series of three tragedies and one satyr play for a single day's showing, for they were judged on the merits of their "package of plays" rather than on individual plays.

After 449 B.C. tragic actors were included in the prize-giving; comic actors were added sometime between 329 and 312 B.C.

The number of comedies produced during part of the fifth century B.C., while the Peloponnesian War was in progress (ca. 428–404 B.C.), was reduced to three. Instead of one day being set aside for comedies, a single comedy was added to the program for each of the three days allocated to tragedies and satyr plays, thereby increasing the total to five plays per day.

In the fourth century B.C. further reductions in the number of plays given and other policy changes were instituted. For example, about 341 B.C. (the earliest record we have) satyr plays were cut from three to one for the entire festival, probably because they had lost much of their earlier appeal. Revivals of fifth-century tragedies were begun in 386 B.C. and of comedies about 339 B.C.

The following century witnessed a further emphasis on revivals of older plays. Contests for them were started in 254 B.C. in the three categories —tragedies, satyr dramas, and comedies. Prizes were also awarded to the best actors in each of them.[3]

City Dionysia ceremonies commenced at dawn, before the actual contests, with offerings, purifications, and other routine functions. This meant that spectators arrived at the theatre in the early morning and remained there most of the day.

The dithyramb and play contests were highly spirited, and the same can be assumed of the awarding of prizes for the best actors, although specific details for the latter are lacking. Great care was exercised to ensure that fairness prevailed. For judging plays, a panel of judges consisting of several men from each of the 10 Attic tribes was drawn up some time before the opening of the festival by the Athenian council *(boulē)* and the participating *choregoi* (producers). The names of several judges nominated by each tribe were inscribed on small, separate tablets and placed in 10 jugs. These were sealed and stored on the Acropolis.

Prior to the opening of the festival, the complete panel of nominated judges was notified of their selection and their attendance on the first day of competitions was requested. On this occasion the jugs were brought into the theatre; the archon (presiding officer) broke the seals and drew one name from each jug. The 10 selected judges stepped forward, were sworn in, and took a solemn oath to render a true verdict to the best of their abilities. When the competitions were completed, the judges cast their ballots for the ones they considered to be the winners by ranking them on their ballots. These were placed in a huge urn provided especially for the purpose. The archon selected at random five of the 10 ballots cast, and these determined the winners.

It is hard to evaluate all the factors which may have influenced a panel of judges in establishing the intrinsic worth of a dramatist's plays. Production elegance—excellent singing and dancing by a well-trained chorus, lavish costumes, sumptuous scenery and properties—could be made possible by a generous *choregos*. They certainly must have been important factors in swaying audience opinion, which, in turn, exerted pressure on the judges. Since the names of the five judges who determined the final outcome of each contest, and how they voted, were made known to all after the contest was over, it may have had some bearing on their voting for a work sponsored by a wealthy, powerful, and influential *choregos*. Also, general audience prejudices—their likes and dislikes, registered in a vociferous manner by the highly volatile theatre audiences—would have had some effect on the judging.

However, the fact that Aeschylus and Sophocles won so many victories indicates that judges, for the most part, were discerning. One notable exception was the defeat of the group of Sophoclean plays containing *Oedipus the King* by a series of plays written by Aeschylus' nephew Philocles, who was considered a mediocre playwright. Either the accompanying plays by Sophocles were inferior, his *choregos* was stingy and failed to mount the plays in a suitable manner, or the judges committed a gross error of judgment; the latter is entirely possible.[4]

TRAGEDIES, COMEDIES, AND SATYR PLAYS IN PRODUCTION

Attention thus far has been directed almost solely to the Lenaea and City Dionysia festivals, with some mention of the Rural Dionysia. The reason is that the bulk of known information comes from Athens and is centered around the fifth and fourth centuries B.C. This is also true when it comes to assembling details on the operational and procedural patterns followed in the staging of productions. However, it is possible to supplement this evidence with additional materials from later festivals given on the island of Delos and other places on the Greek mainland.

PRODUCERS

Theatrical performances in Athens, since they were official civic ceremonies, were conducted and managed by the state *(polis)*. The *archon eponymus* was in charge of the City Dionysia; while the *archon basileus,* the principal religious representative of Athens, administered the Lenaea as well as the celebrated Eleusinian Mysteries. The Rural Dionysia were supervised by the *demarchus* (mayor) of the deme in which the festival was held. Dionysian festivals held at Delos and other centers during the Hellenistic period were managed by an appointed *agonothētēs* (official in charge of festivals) and were financed from their state treasuries.

Each year, several months before the Athenian dramatic festivals were to take place, hopeful playwrights submitted their scripts to the respective archons in charge and applied for a chorus. It was the job of the archons to read all plays as soon as possible and to select from among them the requisite number of playwrights and the best plays to fit the requirements of the festival for that year. A playwright entered his work under his own name, a friend's name, or his son's name. The ruses, however, do not seem to have been successful in concealing the true identity of a playwright.

Choruses were finally granted to the playwrights whose works were deemed worthy to compete at the Lenaea and the City Dionysia. The next step was to provide each of them with a *choregos* (producer). *Choregoi* for the City Dionysia were chosen by lot in July, which gave them plenty of time to prepare their production for the following spring. Since these men paid the salaries and expenses of training and costuming chorus members, flute players, and any mutes or extras to be used, they needed to be wealthy, public-spirited citizens. Actors' salaries were paid by the state.

No doubt the competitive spirit engendered by the festivals led some *choregoi* to spend larger sums of money, perhaps more than they could afford or than was justified. Athens had never been an affluent region, so that the financial burden placed on these men during the fifth century and a greater part of the fourth century B.C. was a heavy drain. In fact, during the year 406–405 B.C. the Peloponnesian War put such a strain on finances that the duties of the *choregos* for tragedy and of the one for comedy were divided between two *choregoi (synchoregoi)*. Sometime between 317 and 307 B.C. *choregoi* in Athens were replaced by an annually elected *agonothētēs*. He was provided with state funds and assumed the duties of a *choregos* for all the playwrights. State subsidy now financed the entire cost of staging theatrical productions. This practice not only was followed in Athens but was extended to all Greek cities almost to the time of their subjugation by Rome.

DIRECTORS AND ACTORS

Thespis, Pratinus, Choerilus, and Phrynichus came close to realizing Edward Gordon Craig's twentieth-century idea of being "artists of the theatre," men who were able to perform all major production tasks with skill and artistry. They wrote the plays, directed them, choreographed the dances, designed the stage settings or furnishings, and filled all the acting roles except that of *koryphaios* (chorus leader). By doubling and tripling in roles, they postponed acting as a separate, distinct profession for 40 years. Aeschylus (ca. 495 B.C.) made the first breakaway when he called upon Cleander to aid him by performing, thereby adding a second actor *(hypokritēs)*. Sophocles (ca. 471–468 B.C.) introduced into tragedy a third and final actor. No more were added except extras and mutes.

The ancient Greeks referred to playwrights as *didaskaloi* (teachers) because they taught the chorus, later the actors, and guided the rehearsals.

When Sophocles gave up acting (ca. 460 B.C.), other playwrights followed his lead and relinquished acting to the new, rising group of skilled actors. Whereas it was usual for tragic playwrights to direct their own works, comic playwrights often had others do it for them. Several of Aristophanes' plays, including *The Banqueters, The Acharnians, Lysistrata, The Wasps, The Frogs,* and *The Birds* were directed by his friends.

When the extant plays of Aristophanes are analyzed to determine the number of actors required to perform them, it appears that in many of them three actors, with the addition of a fourth to play some of the minor speaking roles, are needed, along with one or two mutes.[5] In a few of the plays as many as five speaking actors are essential. Perhaps a similar number were used in Middle and New Comedy, but evidence on this matter is too limited for a firm generalization.

The early extant plays of Aeschylus—*The Persians* (ca. 472 B.C.), *Seven Against Thebes* (467 B.C.), *The Suppliant Maidens* (ca. 463 B.C.?), and *Prometheus Bound* (ca. 460 B.C.?)—were written to be played by a chorus and two actors filling all speaking roles. By changing their masks and costumes and altering their speaking voices, the actors accomplished this without difficulty. The addition of a second actor made it possible for playwrights to extend their plays "in time and space."[6]

With the introduction of the third actor, tragic playwrights were able to present characters in direct conflict, clashing with each other, as Aeschylus did in *The Oresteia* (458 B.C.). Playwriting had by this time made "an unparalleled advance in dramatic expressiveness."[7] Sophocles added further subtleties—plot complications and complex characters—and gave such gifted actors as Tlepolemus, Cleidemides, and Nicostratus vehicles to display their special talents. Euripides demanded of his actors that they be more "human *and* theatrical," both at the same time.[8]

When tragic playwrights gave up playing the lead *(prōtagōnistēs)* in their plays, the choice of replacements for themselves and the second and third players was left under their control. The archon changed this procedure in 449 B.C., when he instituted the practice of selecting three protagonists for tragedy and parceled them out by lot to respective playwrights, requiring each to play in all four of the playwright's works. The second actor *(deuteragōnistēs)* and third actor *(tritagōnistēs)*, who were very much subordinated in their roles to the protagonists, were now engaged by the archon. A few years later a similar method may have been initiated in the acting of comedies.

The growing professional skill of actors and the increased interest in acting on the part of audiences tended to give a marked advantage to the playwright who was lucky enough to have drawn the best protagonist. The system was changed and equalized sometime in the fourth century B.C. by having each protagonist along with his deuteragonist and tritagonist act in a tragedy by every playwright.

The fourth and third centuries B.C. were ablaze with musical and theatrical entertainment. Following the example of Alexander and his successors, rulers vied with one another in lavishly supporting contests, creating new festivals, encouraging the building of new theatres, and renovating and remodeling older theatres. Famous actors traveled extensively and played regularly in the important centers of the Greek world; other performing artists were also in great demand. To bring order and control in the midst of this plenty, artists' guilds began to spring up in the last quarter of the third century B.C. The earliest and most important of these were the Athenian Artists of Dionysus, the Isthmian and Nemean Guild of Corinth, and the Ionia and Hellespont Guild located at Teos in Ionia.

The guilds were federations which included in their membership a wide assortment of artists: playwrights, poets, rhapsodists, chorus members, instrumentalists, costumers, and others. All profited from these organizations, which spread out and finally encompassed the entire Hellenic world. The rising prominence of actors was recognized by the Amphictyonic Decree of about 277 B.C., which gave privileged status to Athenian actors by exempting them from military service and by allowing them freedom to travel in hostile territory in time of war.[9]

Acting developed slowly at first. The earliest playwright-actors were self-taught, but this pattern began to change as soon as acting became a specialized profession. Intensive study and practice were initiated in voice production and body movement, the two essentials for successful acting in the large theatres. By the fourth century B.C. acting had so improved and caught the public fancy that it preempted playwriting in status; with craftsmen taking the place of artists, playwriting slipped into the background, forfeiting prestige.

A good singing and speaking voice was a prime necessity for all actors, followed by years of careful vocal training with emphasis on clear enunciation, resonance, and vocal flexibility. In performance, line delivery varied from plain speech for the sections written in iambic trimeters to recitative backed by flute accompaniment for portions written in tetrameters; lyrical passages were sung to flute accompaniment.

Vocal dexterity was important, for actors shifted back and forth in different characters by doubling and tripling in roles and moved from male to female roles with ease. While all roles were played by men, some actors specialized in playing female parts. Training in bodily movement centered on mastering the system of stylized, symbolic gestures *(cheironomia)* which were used extensively by tragic choruses and adopted by messengers to make their recital of off-stage happenings more vivid. Other actors also used them on occasion.

In the age of Demosthenes great oratory and great acting matured side by side, each contributing to the other. Foremost among the actors was Polus, who played the role of Orestes in Sophocles' *Electra* and, in one of the pivotal scenes, carried an urn containing the ashes of his own son; he used it as an aid to help him convey greater emotional depth in the part. Theodorus was praised for his "natural" style of acting. Neoptolemus, Thessolus, and Athenodorus brought honor and distinction to their profession.

THE CHORUS

When Greek drama was in its most productive period, the chorus was an extremely effective and powerful theatrical instrument. It functioned as an ideal spectator helping audiences and actors to relate emotionally to what was happening in the plays by providing symbolic action that reinforced the relationship. The chorus also continually focused attention where it needed to be directed. The chorus often took an active part in the action of a play by questioning and counseling the characters. The singing, recitative, and dancing of the chorus as they delivered choral odes helped to establish the proper mood to blend in with the action which had just been depicted or was about to be depicted.

By the late fourth century B.C. the chorus was reduced in tragedy and comedy to *embolima,* an interlude status capable of being easily transferred from one play to another. Eventually it could be discarded entirely without much effect on the play.

The size of the tragic chorus *(choreutai)* prior to the advent of Aeschylean drama, which might have used a chorus of 50 in the earliest plays and only 12 in the latest, has not been established. Sophocles increased it to 15 members, where it remained. The *choreutai* in satyr drama numbered 12, while Old Comedy used a chorus of 24 sometimes split into two groups, as in *Lysistrata.* The size and importance of comic choruses dwindled much faster than the others.

Choreutai were amateurs trained and choreographed by playwrights. Later this task was turned over to *chorodidaskaloi* (chorus teachers). Choral discipline was achieved through long and arduous practice in singing the odes and in performing the steps, patterns of movement, and *cheironomia* of the dances. These were accompanied by music composed and played by a single flute player set in various "modes" (for example, Dorian, Phrygian, Lydian, Ionian), which differed from one another in the order of the large and small intervals of which they were composed; furthermore, they could be sung or played in various keys. Each mode had its own particular emotional character *(ēthos)*.[10]

The usual tragic and comic choruses entered singing the *parodos* (entrance song) and led by a flute player. They were grouped in a rectangular marching formation composed of ranks and files—three by five for tragedy and four by six for comedy. Once in position in the orchestra, they turned and faced the spectators, still singing and gesturing.[11] Entrance procedures, however, often varied from this convention according to plot requirements.

During the ensuing episodes the chorus worked out from this formation, reacting with suitable movements and gestures to the unfolding words and actions of characters. The *koryphaios* (chorus leader) entered directly into the action and carried on dialogue with the actors. Choral odes were sung and danced appropriately guided by the meters of the odes. The chorus remained in the orchestra, with a few exceptions, until the play was finished, when it left, marching in rectangular formation.

Choruses in Old Comedy were very active in dancing and singing; some members engaged in dialogue with actors; others at times broke up into smaller groups and sang and danced. The "characteristic dance of Old Comedy was the *kordax.*"[12] It obviously was offensive to a number of persons because some of its movements were lascivious and obscene.

Sileni (horse-men) or satyrs (goat-men) or a blend of the two led by Silenus, an attendant to Dionysus, formed the chorus for satyr drama.[13] Double flute music accompanied the lively and grotesque *sikinnis* (satyric dance).

MASKS

All actors wore masks. It is thought that this feature was a carryover from deity worship as practiced in several parts of ancient Greece. The wearing of masks helped to enhance the mystical quality inherent in theatrical performances. It also made it easier for actors to double in roles. Thespis introduced plain linen masks which were perfected by his successors. The addition of colored and terrifying masks is attributed to Aeschylus. Painted masks with open mouths and attached hair (probably human) suitably arranged for the roles depicted were worn by all actors

Terra-cotta comic mask from Smyrna and tragic mask from Myrino, Hellenistic period, showing high *onkos* and open mouth on both masks and eye holes in tragic mask. (01.7642 and 01.7643, Courtesy, Museum of Fine Arts, Boston.)

Relief of Hellenistic masks showing Menander, seated, holding mask of young man; masks of young woman and older man, on table; standing figure may be personification of Skene (Stage). (Lateran Museum, Rome. Photo Alinari.)

and chorus members. Made of molded, stiffened linen, carved wood, or tooled leather, they were large enough to fit snugly over the actor's entire head, yet were light enough to be worn comfortably. Mask-makers created portrait masks which were often extremely lifelike; the mask of Socrates in *The Clouds* was so realistic that he is reputed to have stood up in the theatre "so that the audience could see his likeness to the actor."[14] They also created masks of historical personages, legendary figures, and gods. Comic and satyr masks were often exaggerated, grotesque, and amusing. Old Comedy choruses of wasps, birds, frogs, and other creatures afforded mask-makers great opportunities for exercising their creative talents.

Information on Hellenistic masks is fairly extensive. Not only did they become conventionalized and stereotyped, but the forehead part *(onkos)* of tragic masks was lengthened. This elongation gave them an archaic appearance and added a few inches of height to the actors who wore them.

In his *Onomasticon* (a thesaurus of terms), Julius Pollux, a Greek scholar and rhetorician of the second century A.D., lists and describes a number of masks. The 28 masks for tragedy he divides into the following categories: 6 for old men, 8 for young men, 3 for male servants, and 11 for women of varying ages. The 44 masks for comedy were divided into: 9 for older men, 11 for younger men, 7 for male servants, and 17 for women of varying ages. To these must be added a whole series of special masks and 4 satyr masks. Fortunately, it is possible to check Pollux's description of several masks against numerous monuments of marble and terra-cotta masks and figurines of actors, mosaics, wall paintings, friezes, and vase paintings—all showing actors wearing masks.

This evidence points up the typing of characters prevalent in Hellenistic and later Roman drama. The age, occupation, and general condition of a character could be determined almost instantly by his or her complexion, contour of face, color and amount of hair, shape of beard, hair-dress, eyebrows, shape and size of mouth, lips, and nose as depicted on the mask.[15]

COSTUMES

The principal actors in classical tragedy wore a woven linen or woolen chiton (tunic) which had wrist-length sleeves, was highly colored and ornamented with designs, and reached to the ground. It was encircled by a girdle worn high, just under the breast. Soft boots laced up the front and a mask covering the face completed the costume, the origins of which may date back to Dionysian and Eleusinian cult worship. But whatever its origin, this type of dress made it easier for men to disguise themselves as

Vase painting (late 5th cent. B.C.) of Euripides' lost play *Andromeda,* according to some authorities. Andromeda wears the sleeved, full-length robe presumably worn by many tragic heroes and heroines. (Courtesy, State Museum of Berlin.)

women because it covered more of the body than did the clothing worn in daily life. It also favored quick costume changes, a necessity for actors doubling in roles. The high-soled boot *(kothornos),* which added a few inches of height to the major tragic actors, came into use in the high-stage Hellenistic theatres.[16] The rather archaic appearance of tragic actors, with their special costumes and masks, helped to lend dignity and awe to their performances.

All minor characters wore ordinary chitons. They consisted of an oblong piece of cloth wrapped or draped around the body. This was the basic dress for everyday wear of men and women alike. The himation (another oblong piece of cloth) was draped over the upper part of the chiton for outdoor wear. Travelers wore the chlamys, a short mantle attached to the left shoulder.

Great use was made of emblems and insignia in costume embellishment

Terra-cotta statuette of Old Comedy angry old man wearing padded, flesh-colored tights; short, belted, heavily padded chiton; and prominent phallus. (Courtesy, State Museum of Berlin.)

Terra-cotta statuettes of Middle Comedy actors: the woman either giggling or weeping behind her himation; the man, wearing a traveler's hat, obviously weeping. (Courtesy, The Metropolitan Museum of Art, Rogers Fund [1913].)

and also of hand properties. Old men carried staffs, and warriors were equipped with armor. Crowns of olive or laurel meant the wearer was bringing good tidings, and crowns of myrtle indicated festivity. Zeus and Athena wore an aegis, a warlike shield or breastplate with a Gorgon's head in the center. Hermes wore winged shoes and carried the caduceus. Hercules (Herakles) appeared in a lion's skin carrying his club. Kings wore crowns and carried sceptres. And Apollo had his bow.[17]

Comic and tragic choruses dressed in a wide variety of costumes suitable for their nationality, occupation, or function in plays. The animal and bird choruses in several of Aristophanes' plays were strikingly costumed.

Sileni and the satyr choruses wore a shaggy undergarment resembling the hide of an animal and equipped with a tail. In addition, the sileni had huge phalluses and often wore animal skins.

Old Comedy actors were provided with a colored, tight-fitting, knit undergarment resembling old-fashioned union-suit underwear. It was grotesquely padded at the belly and the rump. Their chitons were cut short in order to display the red-leather phallus sewn onto the undergarment. Middle and New Comedy actors wore everyday clothing. The colors had symbolic meaning: white was worn by old men and slaves, gray or black indicated parasites, and red or purple was the color for young men.

PRODUCTION AND ACTING STYLES

In performance Greek plays combined dramatic action, poetic dialogue, dancing, and singing. Portions were delivered in spoken dialogue, segments were chanted in recitative, and still other pieces were sung and danced to the accompaniment of flute music. There are some superficial similarities between modern music-dramas or musical comedies and classical Greek plays. However, the latter followed a tighter pattern or structural framework, had a greater thematic thrust, and employed different artistic conventions for each genre. Eventually, the musical and choral portions were subordinated to the dramatic elements, and finally largely disappeared in late tragedy.

Greek tragic acting had simplicity, vigor, and dignity. It contained elements from its ritualistic past as well as certain pageantlike qualities. Clear articulation, careful observance of verse rhythm and meter, appropriate gestures, and skillfully executed movements were qualities ranked highest by audiences.[18] Comic acting was vigorous, lively, and unrestrained. Presentational rather than illusionistic, it was directed to the audience as much as possible.

The production style in ancient Greek theatres must always remain something of a hypothesis. There are, however, a number of specific elements, monuments, and conditions which can lead to the development of such a hypothesis. The following checklist might prove helpful:

1. The texts of extant plays and fragments and what they indicate.

2. The effect the huge outdoor theatres had upon the performers and the performance.

3. The ever-present chorus and how it was handled.

4. The effect doubling and tripling in roles had upon the actors' characterizations.

5. The effect males playing female roles had upon female characterizations.

6. The influence on performers and performances of religious observances and competitive practices at dramatic festivals.

7. The effects of masks on the acting style.

8. The ways in which theatrical performances given in daylight and outdoors, without the advantage of stage lighting or the use of complicated stage machines and scenery, were effected.

DITHYRAMBS AND DORIC MIMES IN PRODUCTION

Dithyrambs were artistic modes of expression which combined choric song, music, and dance given in honor of Dionysus. Participants were boys and men carefully trained to perform material furnished by dithyrambic composers. They did not wear masks. Music for the dithyrambs was furnished by highly skilled flute players. In earlier periods, each chorus consisted of 50 members. Later the number of participants gradually dwindled to 35, 25, 15, 12, 7, 5, and as few as 3 members.[19] Dithyrambs involving several choruses were always presented in competitions. They were eventually given at practically all major festivals celebrated in Greece.

Two dithyrambic competitions were held yearly at the City Dionysia in the fifth century B.C., one featuring 10 choruses of boys and the other 10 choruses of men; each used 50 members chosen by officials representing each of the 10 Attic tribes. Production responsibilities and expenses were assumed by two *choregoi* from each tribe appointed by the archon after receiving tribal endorsement. This meant that there were 10 *choregoi* for the choruses of men and 10 for those of the boys. At first dithyrambic composers took an active role in training choruses and in acting as chorus leaders. Later, when they withdrew from active participation in productions, the *choregoi* hired *didaskaloi* (teacher-directors) and skilled choral leaders.

The little that is known about the production aspects of Doric mimes has been furnished by numerous terra-cotta figurines of actors, vase paintings, and a few clay masks. They indicate that the later Old Comedy costumes of padded undergarment, phallus, short tunic, grotesque mask, and animal mask had their origin in these forms of entertainment.

STAGE SCENERY AND MACHINERY

Theatrical scenic elements used in staging early plays were limited at first to altars, tombs, rocks, hills, benches, and statues of gods. Stage properties consisted of dummies, biers, couches, and chariots.

When temporary wooden scene buildings were added at the Theatre of Dionysus sometime before 460 B.C., they could be used, when needed, to represent a palace, a temple, or a dwelling. Scene painting may have been introduced by Sophocles, or earlier by Agatharchus for a series of plays presented by Aescyhlus. It seems logical to assume that painted scenery on some kind of frame was not used prior to the introduction of the scene building. It may be that the early scene-painters, instead of painting the scenery, merely decorated the scene building.[20] Painted scenery as we know it was probably unknown in the classical period.

Pericles' renovation of the Theatre of Dionysus about 445 B.C. made it possible and much easier to change the *skene,* which became a temporary wooden structure erected in front of the long stoa facing the orchestra. The rear section of the *skene* was supported by timbers placed in the 10 stone slots located in the retaining wall which supported the south side of the orchestra terrace. Presumably, the *skene* became more elaborate later.

Lycurgus replaced the "Periclean Theatre" of Dionysus about 338–326 B.C. with a permanent stone *skene* with *paraskenia,* a decorative *proskenion,* and stone seats.

Painted scene panels *(pinakes)* made of wood or hides, similar to today's muslin stage "flats," were introduced in Hellenistic theatres. They could be fastened into position between the columns fronting the scene building which supported the stage, special niches in the stone columns being provided for this purpose. This arrangement can be verified by examination of remaining columns found in several theatres. *Pinakes* might also have furnished scenic backing for scenes staged in the *thyromata.*

Both Pollux and Vitruvius imprecisely describe three-sided, prismlike contrivances called *periaktoi* which revolved on pivots and were fitted with changeable scenic panels. They were probably located near the side entrances to the stage in Hellenistic theatres. Bieber thinks there is evidence to support this hypothesis at the Theatre of Elis, Pergamum, and Dionysus.[21] The *periaktoi* were seemingly capable of indicating locale changes when turned and also displayed appropriate symbols when gods appeared.

In the latter part of the fifth century B.C. the theatre started moving in the direction of spectacle and away from its former simplicity. It was aided by the addition of stage machines, the *mēchanē* and the *ekkyklema*. To these should be added "Charon's steps" (underground tunnels), a *keraunoskopeion* (lightning machine), a *bronteion* (thunder machine), and a few more special devices listed by Pollux but so scantily described that it is impossible to determine their specific modes of operation.

The *mēchanē* was a cranelike piece of stage equipment with ropes and pulleys which was used to fly or transport actors in comedies and tragedies from the roof of the *skene* to the acting area below. How it operated, its degree of sophistication, and whether it was located behind and to one side of the *skene* or on top of it cannot be established. It came into use after about 430 B.C.,[22] particularly in the plays of Euripides (see Line 1231 of *Andromache* for a specific example of its use). Aristophanes used the *mēchanē* in *The Clouds* when he suspended Socrates between heaven and earth in a basket.

The *ekkyklema* was a movable platform which operated on rollers and was of a size capable of clearing the doorways of the scene buildings, or it might have revolved on large hinges fastened to the central doorway. "Dreadful actions committed indoors" were wheeled or swung out on it for the audience to view. The *ekkyklema* may have been used as early as in *Agamemnon* to display the murdered bodies of Agamemnon and Cassandra with Clytemnestra standing over them. This scene occurs at Line 1372. Other examples of its possible uses are to be found in *The Libation Bearers*, *Ajax*, *Hippolytus*, and the *Electra* of Sophocles and of Euripides. Aristophanes probably employed it in two of his extant comedies, *The Acharnians* and *The Thesmophoriazusae*.

The Hellenistic theatres of Eretria, Sicyon, Magnesia, Tralles, Syracuse, and Segesta show evidence of "Charon's steps,"[23] underground passageways extending from within the scene building to the middle of the orchestra and used by ghosts and other characters who needed to make sudden entrances in the orchestra area. It is not known whether these passageways were used prior to the Hellenistic period.

AUDIENCES

One of the critical factors to be considered in determining the caliber of theatrical offerings for any given culture is its taste or lack of taste, judgments passed on its plays by assembled theatre audiences which are made up of the ignorant as well as the learned. Athenian audiences followed the action depicted in plays intently, applauded vigorously what they liked, vociferously rejected what they did not like. Plays could even be stopped in performance if specific content or inept execution offended enough people in the audience. "Wise and noble sentiment,"[24] fine acting, and good chorus work were much appreciated.

If it were possible for us to project ourselves back in time, to attend a series of performances at one of the great festivals given in the Theatre of Dionysus, the strongest impressions we would have, aside from those caused by strange scenic and acting conventions, would be of the audience. For they were caught up in a feverish excitement, an intense interest in the outcome of the various contests. Their volatility and enthusiasm were more characteristic of present-day football and baseball spectators than of the quiet, decorous, often passive demeanor exhibited by our theatre audiences. The hundreds directly competing for prizes and honors in the City Dionysia sharpened the appetite for victory. Add to this group several hundred, perhaps several thousand, former chorus members, dithyrambic performers, flute players, and extras sprinkled among the audience. They had competed in previous festivals and were quite knowledgeable on the finer points and techniques of performance. Refreshments to sustain the "dawn to dusk" audience were hawked, thereby increasing the general noise and commotion.

The performances were free-wheeling, presented with gusto and great fervor for the enjoyment of everybody. Audiences could easily pass in a single day from the noblest tragedy to the absurdities and grossness of Old Comedy and to the licentious merriment of a satyr drama which may have burlesqued the heroic figures just presented in a tragedy; obviously they enjoyed each with equal relish. Direct address to the audience and the *parabasis* in Old Comedy which was concerned with political matters must have elicited especially sharp vocal reactions from members in the audience.

Audiences included a few women, boys, and slaves, but were predominately adult males. Many foreigners, visiting dignitaries, and Greek colonists from abroad were in attendance at the City Dionysia, for Athens was proud of showing off its latest artistic creations. Since the seating capacity of the Theatre of Dionysus was reached at about

17,000 persons, possibly 20,000 or more with standees, about one-eighth of the estimated 155,000 citizen, slave, and alien resident population of Periclean Athens[25] in 430 B.C. was in attendance on any one day of a dramatic festival.

Admission to the City Dionysia was free in the earliest period, but sometime in the fifth century B.C. two obols per day was charged to help keep the theatre in repair. Later a theoric fund (theatre money) was created to pay for admission at first for those in financial need, later to all who applied for it, needy or not. This public outlay of funds became a much disputed matter and was abolished near the end of the Peloponnesian War, only to be reinstated later. It was finally stopped permanently by Demosthenes about 338 B.C. because it was said to have overburdened the resources of government in time of war.

Specimens of theatre tickets made of bronze and terra-cotta, but mostly of lead, and resembling stamped coins with emblems and numbers have been found in various parts of the Greek world.[26]

Privileged persons (priests, archons, generals, high officials, public benefactors, and visiting notables) were granted seats of honor in all Greek theatres. These could be benches with backs or specially designated throne seats most often located directly adjoining the orchestra. The general public always sat on backless benches, no doubt made more comfortable by blankets and cushions.

Theatregoing increased rapidly in the Hellenistic age, when every important urban center was provided with a theatre or a theatre-odeion complex and numerous festivals featuring plays sprang up in numerous places on the mainland of Greece, the Aegean islands, Turkey, Sicily, southern Italy, and North Africa.

NOTES

1. Detailed information on dramatic festivals held in Greece, particularly Athens, is to be found in the following works: James Turney Allen, *Stage Antiquities of the Greeks and Romans and their Influence* (New York: Longmans, Green, 1927), pp. 30–49; Margarete Bieber, *The History of the Greek and Roman Theater* (2nd ed. rev. and enlarged; Princeton, N.J.: Princeton University Press, 1961), pp. 51–53; Roy C. Flickinger, *The Greek Theatre and Its Drama* (4th ed.; Chicago: University of Chicago Press, 1936), pp. 196–220; A. E. Haigh, *The Attic Theatre* (3rd ed. rev. in part rewritten by Sir Arthur W. Pickard-Cambridge; Oxford: Clarendon Press, 1907), pp. 1–77; and the definitive work on the subject, Sir Arthur W. Pickard-Cambridge, *The Dramatic Festivals of Athens* (Oxford: Clarendon Press, 1953; 2nd ed. by John Gould and D. M. Lewis, 1968).

2. G. M. Sifakis, *Studies in the History of Hellenistic Drama* (London: University

of London, Athlone Press, 1967), p. 1. Sifakis deals with the dramatic festivals held in Delos and Delphi.

3. A chronological listing of dates for changes in the procedures at the City Dionysia and Lenaea is given in Pickard-Cambridge, *op. cit.* (1st ed.), p. 73.

4. Fairly extensive accounts of the judging mechanism for the City Dionysia are found in Haigh, *op. cit.*, pp. 31–48, and Pickard-Cambridge, *op. cit.* (1st ed.), pp. 96–126.

5. Pickard-Cambridge, *op. cit.* (1st ed.), pp. 148–153.

6. Gerald F. Else, *The Origin and Early Form of Greek Tragedy* (Cambridge, Mass.: Harvard University Press, 1965), p. 86.

7. Albin Lesky, *Greek Tragedy* (trans. by H. A. Frankfort with a foreword by E. G. Turner; London: Ernest Benn, 1965), p. 60.

8. Edwin Duerr, *The Length and Depth of Acting* (with a foreword by A. M. Nagler; New York: Holt, Rinehart and Winston, 1962), p. 25. The section on ancient Greek acting, pp. 9–38, is very perceptive and should be consulted.

9. Pickard-Cambridge, *op. cit.* (1st ed.), pp. 286–319, deals in detail with "The Artists of Dionysus."

10. Lillian B. Lawler, *The Dance of the Ancient Greek Theatre* (Iowa City: University of Iowa Press, 1964), p. 24. For additional information on the chorus, see Haigh, *op. cit.*, pp. 283–322; H. D. F. Kitto, "The Greek Chorus," *Educational Theatre Journal*, 9 (1956), 1–8; and Pickard-Cambridge, *op. cit.* (1st ed.), pp. 239–267.

11. Lawler, *op. cit.*, p. 28.

12. *Ibid.*, p. 69.

13. *Ibid.*, p. 103.

14. See T. B. L. Webster, *Greek Theatre Production* (London: Methuen, 1956), p. 60.

15. For additional information on Greek masks, consult A. M. Nagler, *A Source Book in Theatrical History* (New York: Dover Publications, 1959), pp. 7–15; Allardyce Nicoll, *The Development of the Theatre* (5th ed. rev.; London: George G. Harrap, 1966), pp. 27–37; Pickard-Cambridge, *op. cit.* (1st ed.), pp. 177–212; and Webster, *op. cit.*, pp. 35–96.

16. Webster, *op. cit.*, p. 44.

17. Haigh, *op. cit.*, p. 252.

18. See James Turney Allen, "Greek Acting in the Fifth Century," *University of California Publications in Classical Philology*, 2 (1916), 279–289.

19. Lawler, *op. cit.*, p. 21.

20. See Peter D. Arnott, *Greek Scenic Conventions in the Fifth Century B.C.* (Oxford: Clarendon Press, 1962), p. 94.

21. Bieber, *op. cit.*, p. 75.

22. Nicoll, *op. cit.*, p. 21.

23. William Bell Dinsmoor, *The Architecture of Ancient Greece: An Account of Its Historic Development* (3rd ed. rev.; London: B. T. Batsford, 1950), p. 314.

24. Haigh, *op. cit.*, p. 346.

25. See A. R. Burn, *The Pelican History of Greece* (Baltimore: Penguin Books, 1966), p. 215. An excellent short history of Greece.

26. See Pickard-Cambridge, *op. cit.* (1st ed.), pp. 273–275, for pictures of ancient Greek theatre tickets; see also pp. 270–272 (2nd ed.), where it is pointed out that all theatre tickets were made of lead.

4

ROMAN THEATRE: DRAMA AND OTHER FORMS

Indigenous improvised theatrical performances were given in early Italy long before any literary drama developed. Later, as other forms of improvised theatre came into being, they were heavily influenced by the Dorian Greeks who had colonized parts of southern Italy and Sicily in the middle of the eighth century B.C. (Cumae was founded about 750 B.C. and Syracuse about 734 B.C.) When literary drama finally appeared in Rome in 240 B.C., it consisted of Greek plays translated and adapted into Latin. Eventually a new important theatrical genre emerged—Roman pantomime.

No real lack of theatrical entertainment existed in Rome during a large portion of the Republic era and for most of the Empire period. The quality and value of the theatrical offerings raises questions that will be commented upon later.

The starting point for a partial account of the beginnings of theatre in Italy is to be found in Book Seven of Livy's *History of Rome*.[1]

ETRUSCAN DANCES AND FESCENNINE VERSES

Two types of early, very rudimentary theatre originated, perhaps as early as the sixth century B.C., in and around Etruria, the region of western Italy between the Arno River on the north, the Tiber River on the south, and the Apennines on the east. The Etruscan civilization that developed there had a strong influence on particular aspects of Roman culture. One of the theatrical forms that originated in Etruria consisted of crude, bantering, improvised verses often sung. These were later called Fescennine verses. The other form featured religious dances performed to music furnished by flute players. These were given at funerals and at festivals honoring the gods.

A group of these Etruscan dancers brought the inhabitants of Rome their first contact with dramatic entertainment. They were invited to Rome in 364 B.C. by the ultraconservative consuls to appease the wrath of the gods and to persuade them to withdraw a pestilence which many thought had been inflicted by these deities. According to Livy, the Roman youths were very much attracted to the Etruscan dances and amplified them by adding improvised dialogue and gestures. The participants in these new entertainments were called *histriones,* a term derived from the Etruscan word *ister* (player).

Fescennine verses grew out of rural festive occasions celebrating successful harvests and were especially given at the feast of Silvanus, an old Italian divinity and protector of fields, gardens, and cattle. They were also popular at weddings, for it was thought that they helped to avert misfortune. The crude, improvised verses were delivered in meter, often sung in a most suggestive and graphic manner, and hurled back and forth by the performers—much to the delight of those watching. The verses may have received their name from the small Etruscan village of Fescennium, or from *fascinum* (black magic), for they were supposed to possess magical powers.[2]

SATURAE

Another form of early Italian theatrical entertainment mentioned by Livy and one that has caused much debate was the satura. Presumably, it consisted of a mixture or medley of dances, improvised songs, and farcical sketches without plots. The satura probably resembled the Fescennine verses but with more accent on the musical and danced portions.

ATELLAN FARCES

The *fabula Atellana* (Atellan farce or comedy) was a native form of Italian theatre that emerged sometime between 350 and 300 B.C. and is usually credited as being a product of the Oscans of Campania (the region around Naples). It received its name from the ancient town of Atella situated not far from Capua on the road from Naples to Rome. However, there is good reason to believe that the Greek *phlyakes* (farces) of Magna Graecia and Sicily had a strong influence on them. If this were true, these farces could have originated anywhere in southern Italy, perhaps even Sicily, before moving into the Campania.

The short Atellan farces were originally given in the Oscan dialect and featured, at first, improvised dialogue, song, music, dance, and a set of stock characters always wearing masks. The crude stock farcical situations were based on drinking, gluttony, thievery, disguise, and many forms of intrigue. Later, when the Atellan farces moved to Rome, they were given in Latin. The dialogue for them began to be written out by at least the first

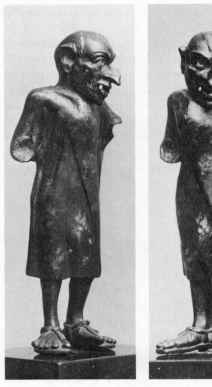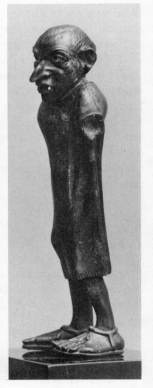

Three views of bronze statuette (300–100 B.C.) of Atellan-farce character Dossenus (The Chewer) showing large mask with big ears, huge, crooked nose, and prominent teeth. (Courtesy, The Metropolitan Museum of Art, Rogers Fund [1912].)

century B.C. Knowledge concerning these farces comes from scenes painted on vases, small terra-cotta and bronze statuettes and masks, written fragments, and play titles. The play titles often contained the names of the stock characters: *Maccus the Soldier*, *Bucco the Gladiator*, and *The Bride of Pappus*. Other titles suggested a more rustic setting: *The Sow* and *The She-Goat*. Still other titles indicated a racy treatment of sexual matters: *The Pimp* and *The Brothel*.

The four stock characters of Oscan masks were Maccus (The Stupid), the leading actor of the group who was a greedy glutton; Bucco (The Fool), a fat-cheeked, talkative, gluttonous braggart; Pappus (The Grandfather), an old man frequently deceived by his wife or daughter; and Dossenus or Manducus (The Chewer), a hump-backed character depicted with a large-jawed, toothy mask indicative of his gluttony.

The appeal of the Atellan farces for the Roman populace was far greater than that of literary comedy and tragedy. Its basic core of topical allusions, intrigue, crudity (sometimes of an obscene nature), and buffoonery set it apart from other forms of entertainment and helped to keep it in tune with the tastes of its audience. This fact is attested by the many references to Atellan farces in the works of prominent Roman writers.

The names of a few of the playwrights who wrote Atellan farces are known, and the titles of more than 100 of them and more than 400 lines and fragments of lines are extant. Pomponius of Bononia and Novius, who wrote in the early part of the first century B.C., specialized in this form of dramatic writing. It reached its peak with them and reverted to its improvised pattern during the later Empire. The Atellan farces were given for several centuries, possibly down to the very end of the Roman Empire, but continued to lose ground to the more popular Roman mimes and lingered on mainly as afterpieces.[3]

MIMES

The most popular form of theatre in the Republic and throughout the Empire, certainly the most enduring form developed by the Romans, was the mime (Latin *mimus*, from Greek *mimos*, akin to *mimesthai* to imitate), a term which could be applied to either the play or the player.

At a very early date, perhaps in the fifth century B.C., the Greeks brought Doric mimes into their colonies in southern Italy (Magna Graecia) and Sicily. During the Pyrrhic War (275–272 B.C.), fought in southern Italy, the Romans came into contact with these Greek mimes and evidently found them much to their liking, for Greek mimes were highly skilled in the art of gesture and mimicry.

From the very beginning the Italian mimes were specialty performers, skilled in a variety of ways—dancing, singing, acrobatics, juggling, and other entertainments. Above all, they were excellent in the art of imitation. The Greek influence of improvisation led these performers into creating improvised sketches that soon began to dominate their work. But like the later Commèdia dell'Arte players, all their special skills were incorporated into their productions.

The rapid growth of Italian mimes is attested by the establishment in Rome in 238 B.C. of the Ludi Florales games which featured them. The Italian mimes at first depended on improvised dialogue. Decimus Laberius (106–43 B.C.) is credited with being the first to give mimes a written form. A number of the titles and fragments of his mimes are extant.

There were no stock characters in the mimes, and the actors, for the most part, did not employ masks. Female roles were played by women. Since the mime plays and players imitated life so closely, references are found in antiquity to their lascivious nature both in actions and words and to some of the grotesque dances. The farcical situations often bordered on the indecent; adultery or attempted adultery and unnatural vices were favorite themes. The plays were scattered with topical allusions. Emphasis was always on character and situation. The players were after laughs and amusement, often of a low order; plot was of secondary importance. Some authorities believe that at one time Plautus may have acted in mimes. Certainly some of the comic business in his plays may well have come from his contact with mimes rather than from the Greek comedies he translated and adapted for the Roman stage. Mimes were a true reflection of the tastes of a large segment of the Roman public. They remained vigorous throughout the Imperial times, increased in popularity, and lasted down to the beginning of the Middle Ages.

PANTOMIMES

The last major theatrical genre to emerge out of Roman culture, and the most important original contribution the Romans made to theatrical art, was the pantomimic dance, or pantomime. It was performed by a *pantomimus* (masked dancer) who acted out stories by means of expressive, rhythmic body movements and gestures while the words of the story were sung by a vocalist accompanied by a lone flute player. Later, the single vocalist was replaced by a chorus accompanied by a small orchestra. The *pantomimus* depicted several roles in succession, and probably wore a different mask for each role. The masks featured closed mouths in contrast to the open-mouthed ones worn by actors in the comedies, tragedies, and Atellan farces.

Pantomimes were first developed in Magna Graecia, the seedbed for much of the early theatrical activity in Italy. About 22 B.C., during the reign of Augustus Caesar, Pylades the Cilician and Bathyllus from Alexandria introduced this new art into Rome, where it achieved great popularity during the Empire.

The composers of pantomimes took their basic stories from the Greek world of myth and legend, especially the love stories of gods and goddesses and the heroic love tales. The pantomime based on *Leda and the Swan* became extremely popular. Because of the subject matter of the pantomimes, the audiences needed to be knowledgeable in mythology and to have an appreciation for the subtleties and finer points of dancing to enjoy them fully. Their appeal was strongest in the higher echelons of Roman society, where the most avid followers were to be found, especially among women. Since the more sensuous and erotic elements predominated in pantomime, they were condemned by many on the grounds of being immoral and having an evil influence upon people.

PHLYAKES

Not to be considered in the mainstream of Roman drama were a series of improvised farces, *phlyakes,* developed by the Greeks in Magna Graecia and Sicily during the fourth and third centuries B.C. They dealt with comic situations taken from daily life and burlesques based on mythical materials or mythical treatments of popular tragedies. Knowledge of the *phlyake* farces (gossips) has been derived principally from a large number of vase paintings in southern Italy that depict scenes from these plays.

The *phlyake* mythological burlesque *hilarotragodia* (hilarious tragedy) achieved its literary form at the hands of Rhinthon of Tarentum around 300 B.C. The vase paintings, all of which date from a prior period (fourth century B.C.), give much information on the stock characters and the costumes worn by the actors, together with some indication of the situations used in the plays, the stages, and the staging employed. These

Drawing from *phlyake* vase painting of father and son fighting over a woman. (From Dörpfeld and Reisch, *Griechische Theater* [1896].)

portable wooden stages had a marked influence on the staging of early literary drama in Rome.[4]

TRAGIC RECITATIONS

Recitations given by single actors of tragic scenes from popular Greek and Roman tragedies came into fashion in Rome during the first century A.D. and lasted down to the fifth century A.D. They started when tragedy as a creative art went into eclipse since new tragedies were not being written and produced. Not much is known about the actual mechanics of these performances. It is known that the actors wore full costumes and masks, and recited, sang, or mimed the roles. If mimed, a vocalist accompanied by an orchestra sang the lines while the actor went through the appropriate movements and gestures. Nero favored these kinds of performances and prided himself on his ability to sing a variety of roles, male and female.

PYRRHIC DANCES

Pyrrhic dances, which had originated in Greece in the form of mimic sham battles engaged in by armed soldiers, were converted by the Imperial Romans into dramatic dances. The participants, both men and women, representing satyrs, maenads, and other colorful beings, fought battles based on mythological happenings, such as the legend of Dionysus, the judgment of Paris, the adventures of Bacchus in some exotic land, and the doom of Pentheus. They resembled lavishly costumed ballets. Pyrrhic dances of a more realistic and grotesque nature were given occasionally in the Colosseum by specially trained criminals.

TRAGEDIES AND COMEDIES

Roman arts and crafts, most particularly the art of the theatre, received a much-needed impetus in the third century B.C., when the first great war with Carthage (the First Punic War, 264–241 B.C.—Punic was the language spoken by the Carthaginians) was fought in Sicily. Young Roman soldiers were brought into direct contact with the flourishing Greek civilization. They were billeted in Sicilian towns and in the suburbs of the larger cities. Their long military hitches lasted six or more years, which gave them abundant opportunities to acquire at least a smattering of the Greek language. Since every city of any size in Sicily had a theatre presenting a variety of offerings—Greek tragedies, Greek New Comedies, Doric mimes, and *phlyakes*—these Roman soldiers in their off-hours from military duties must have developed a taste for Greek theatre. It is not surprising, then, that in the year following the end of the First Punic War (240 B.C.) literary drama finally reached Rome. The production of Greek tragedies and comedies in Latin adaptations was incorporated into the activities of the Ludi Romani. This move had been helped along by the returning army veterans and by the large number of Greek slaves captured earlier at Tarentum (272 B.C.) who had been tutoring the children of wealthy Romans for several years and developing in them a taste for Greek literature, especially for plays.

The credit for translating, adapting, and producing the first Greek plays in Latin goes to a Romanized Greek by the name of Livius Andronicus (ca. 284–204 B.C.), born perhaps in Tarentum, a Greek-settled coastal city in Calabria, Italy. Since Tarentum supported a thriving theatre, he probably received a very good background in all phases of theatre. His arrival in Rome and other details surrounding his personal life, such as his being a slave and later freed and his tutoring in a house bearing the name of Livius, are speculative. Andronicus busied himself in the years between 240 and 207 B.C. translating Homer's *Odyssey* into Latin, as well as translating and adapting several Greek tragedies and Greek New Comedies.

All that exists of his work today are the titles of eight tragedies and three comedies. For his first assignment in 240 B.C., he furnished a tragedy and a comedy for the Ludi Romani. Besides translating the plays, he composed the musical portions *(cantica)* for the comedies which were given in some form of recitative with a musical accompaniment. He also produced them and acted in them. Andronicus' work marked a most important development for the Roman theatre.

Gnaeus Naevius (ca. 270–201 B.C.), a few years younger than Livius Andronicus, is regarded as Italy's first native dramatist. By birth a Campanian, he later became a Roman citizen. All evidence about him bears out the fact that he showed a great deal of originality as well as independence in his writing. He was a veteran of the First Punic War and it was then that he first came into contact with the Greek theatre. There is a reference to the effect that one of his early plays, if not his earliest, was given at the public games in Rome, probably the Ludi Romani in 235 B.C. The remains of his work today consist of the titles of seven of the nine tragedies he wrote, 34 titles of his comedies, and 190 lines and fragments. Naevius also created a new form of drama based on events in Roman history: the historical play *(fabula praetexta)*. The name was derived from the purple-bordered toga worn by magistrates. Two of his plays, *Romulus*, dealing with the legendary past of Rome, and *Clastidium*, based on a famous contemporary military victory in 222 B.C., belong in this category. The *fabula praetexta* never achieved great popularity; only a few were ever written. Toward the end of his career, about 206 B.C., Naevius was imprisoned for two years because of the attack in one of his plays on the Metelli and their consulship.

In the 22 years between the First and Second Punic Wars the newly Latinized Greek plays did a brisk business in Rome. Theatre festivals were curtailed to some extent during the Second Punic War (218–202 B.C.) because they placed a heavy drain on Roman material resources and manpower, when every effort was being made to defeat Hannibal. However, during the early part of the war, Rome formed a coalition with several Greek states to prevent the Macedonians from aiding the Carthaginians. This movement helped to encourage the theatre as well as Greco-Roman art. With the end of the war a countermovement led by

Cato opposed what it considered to be the harmful, insidious, effete Greek influences creeping into Roman culture. This latter movement, coupled with the general conservatism of the Romans, blocked the building of any permanent theatre buildings in Rome until 55 B.C.

In the middle years of the second century B.C. Roman armies began moving into the eastern kingdoms. This abrupt contact with Hellenistic culture sent a number of distinguished Greeks—philosophers, scientists, writers—scurrying to Rome as envoys to represent their kingdoms and plead their cases. At the same time, an increasing quantity of highly educated Greek slaves and hostages were brought to Rome to serve as tutors and advisers. These factors helped to counter and offset the full effect of the anti-Greek movement in its attempt to choke off theatre in Rome. As a result, Rome experienced its "Golden Age of Drama," a period that lasted from approximately 200 to 85 B.C.

The work of three outstanding dramatists who specialized in writing tragedies falls within this period: Ennius, Pacuvius, and Accius. Unfortunately, their plays are only known by titles and fragments and from com-

Terra-cotta statuettes of *fabula praetexta* actors in Roman dress: possible money-lender, possible politician, and potter. (Courtesy, Trustees of the British Museum.)

ments about their work by their contemporaries and by later Roman writers.

Quintus Ennius (239–169 B.C.), born in southern Italy, was a veteran of the Second Punic War, a writer, teacher, and dramatist. He was brought to Rome by Cato in 204 B.C. Besides the titles for two comedies and two *fabulae praetextae*, there are titles for 20 of his tragedies, mostly drawn from the plays of Euripides, whose work had great appeal for him. The more than 400 extant fragments of his plays indicate that he may have retained the Greek choral form in his translations.

Marcus Pacuvius (ca. 220–130 B.C.), the combination painter and dramatist, was born at Brundisium (Brindisi) but spent most of his life in Rome. He specialized in the writing of tragedies, of which 12 titles and one title of a *praetexta* and 400 lines remain. Cicero and Quintilian ranked Pacuvius, along with Accius, as the best of the Roman tragic playwrights. His plays were popular long after his death. He was also a grammarian as well as a literary critic.

Lucius Accius (170–ca. 86 B.C.) was the last but the most productive of the Roman tragic playwrights, having written more than 40 tragedies. He is also credited with two *fabulae praetextae*—*Aencodae*, or *Decius*, and *Brutus*. About 700 lines and fragments of his work are extant, enough to give some idea of his writing abilities. The longest fragment consists of 12 lines from his *Medea*.

Before the disappearance of tragic playwriting, a number of dabblers and one prominent philosopher-teacher tried their hand at writing tragedies. Their work, with a single exception, is known in such a limited way that mere mention of them is about all that is possible. There were C. Julius Strabo (?–87 B.C.), a prominent orator; C. Titus, a Roman knight; Pompilius Santra, a grammarian; Rufus Varius, the author of *Thyestes*, performed in 29 B.C.; L. Pomponius Secundus, who may have been the last Roman to write a tragedy for stage production; and Ovid, who wrote a *Medea* but there is no record of its having been performed or even written with a stage performance in mind. The major evidence now supports the contention that the nine extant tragedies of Seneca (ca. 4 B.C.– 65 A.D.)—*The Mad Hercules, The Trojan Women, The Phoenician Women, Medea, Phaedra, Oedipus, Thyestes, Agamemnon, Hercules on Oeta*—were written to be recited, perhaps in a manner similar to the current reader's theatre presentations, rather than to be given as fully staged productions.

The throttling of tragedy was completed in the Empire period by a combination of forces: the increasing presence of deteriorating influences in the leading forms of entertainment; the withdrawal of the more educated and literary classes from the theatre; the movement in the direction of writing "closet tragedies" rather than "stage tragedies"; the ever-widening interest in theatrical spectacle, brought about by the desires of theatrical producers to fill the huge stages of the new stone theatres of Rome in a fitting manner, much to the detriment of other elements in the productions; and finally, an ironclad censorship which blocked that freedom of expression so desperately needed if theatre at any time or any place is to thrive.

It is difficult to judge the effectiveness of Roman tragedies because the evidence is scanty and has to be based entirely on the fragmentary testimony of ancient critics and grammarians and on the still more fragmentary collection of lines, bits of plays, and titles. Most scholars feel that it was vigorous, filled with oratorical passages, but weak in character delineations.

The general effectiveness of Roman comedy is much easier to evaluate because 20 of the comedies written by Plautus and the total output of six comedies written by Terence are extant.

There were a great number of Roman dramatists, besides the ones already mentioned, who specialized in *fabulae palliatae* (comedies in Greek dress). The best-known of these was Caesilius Statius (ca. 219–166 B.C.), who authored at least 42 known comedies for which titles and fragments exist. There are several more dramatists of this same "titles and fragments" class which fails to furnish much of a basis for judging the importance of their work. The same can be said for the three known comedy writers of *fabulae togatae* (comedies in native dress)—Titinius, Afranius, and Alta. There are 70 titles and a string of fragments, odds and ends of lines from various plays. These plays, as nearly as can be determined, were popular with the audiences at the time when they were first produced.

Roman drama had a tremendous influence on Renaissance playwrights, who looked to the plays of Seneca for examples of rhetorical display, moral philosophizing, horror, mythological lore, and mystical concerns with the underworld. The surviving plays of Plautus and Terence furnished models for later comic writers to copy and imitate as well as models for Renaissance scholars to use in teaching spoken Latin.

PLAUTUS

Titus Maccius Plautus (ca. 254–ca. 184 B.C.) was born in the small Umbrian village of Sarsina. Titus was the name given to him by his father; Plautus ("Flatfoot") he earned as a nickname; and he may have acquired Maccius because of his skill at playing the role of Maccus in Atellan farces.

He was a young man when he came to Rome, where presumably he found work as a stage helper and part-time actor in plays and Atellan farces. While he was doing this he must have spent a considerable amount of time learning Greek and familiarizing himself with Greek New Comedies.

The surviving plays of Plautus clearly indicate that he possessed a thorough knowledge and understanding of the craftsmanship of all phases of theatre. The evidence data are slim concerning his supposed business venture, shipping, in which he lost all his money when the loaded vessel he had chartered sank in a storm. He was thus reduced to labor, grinding corn in a mill to earn a living. It was most likely that Plautus joined the army for a six-year stretch when Hannibal threatened Rome (ca. 220 B.C.). Almost every available man in Rome physically able was used to repel this invasion.

Plautine comedies are filled with military terms picked up, no doubt, from his long army service. Plautus was at least in his late thirties, perhaps early forties, when he began his career as a comic playwright, but by then he was well prepared for his task. His keen observation of all kinds of people, his long period of apprenticeship in the theatre, and his awareness of what it took to entertain a Roman audience are clearly demonstrated in his plays. He was a master of wit, plotting, and farcical situations. Above all, the Greek originals of his plays were not slavishly imitated.

The four best-known Plautine plays are *Amphitryon*, based on an amusing situation which each age has found fascinating; *Miles Gloriosus* (*The Braggart Warrior*), with its superb debunking of a would-be military hero and lady-killer; *Menaechmi* (*The Twin Menaechmi*), which so successfully exploits mistaken identity; and *Aulularia* (*The Pot of Gold*), which delights with its humorous and not so humorous treatment of a miser and his daughter. The other plays of Plautus which have survived are *The Comedy of Asses*, *Two Bacchides*, *The Captives*, *Casina*, *The Casket*, *Curculio*, *Epidicus*, *The Merchant*, *The Haunted House*, *The Persian*, *The Carthaginian*, *Pseudolus*, *Rope*, *Stichus*, *Trinummus*, and *Truculentus*.[5]

TERENCE

Few playwrights have been more popular long after their death than during their lifetime. This honor fell to Terence (Publius Terentius Afer, ca. 185/4–159 B.C.), who was born in Carthage. Arriving in Rome as a slave when quite young, he was well educated by his master—a Roman senator named Terentius Lucanus—and was later freed (manumitted). Terence was welcomed into the intellectual Roman taste-makers' circle of literary men and wrote six polished comedies that met with their approval.

These plays also won a large reading audience for him in the Middle Ages and Renaissance. However, his work was bitterly assailed by his contemporaries, particularly the playwrights.

He defended himself in the prologues to his plays and pleaded for a fair hearing from his audiences. He refuted the criticisms directed at him for contamination (combining two or more Greek originals) by citing other Roman playwrights who had done the same thing; denied the charges of theft and plagiarism for his plays; upheld his friendships with other literary figures; and met the accusation of weakness in his writing style by directing the same charge against his attackers. Terence died in Greece in 159 B.C.; some think he drowned at sea on a return trip to Rome. He had been visiting Greece in search of more plays to translate and adapt and probably to get some first-hand knowledge of the country.

The comedies of Terence were all produced within a seven-year period (166–160 B.C.). *Andria* (*The Woman of Andros*), *Heauton Timorumenos* (*The Self-Tormentor*), *Eunuchus* (*The Eunuch*), and *Hecyra* (*The Mother-in-Law*) were given at the Ludi Megalenses. The second prologue for *The Mother-in-Law* indicates that it suffered two unsuccessful performances when audiences walked out on it. The first time, the theatre was emptied by a rumor that rope dancers and boxers were performing at another place. The second time it was given, at the Ludi Funebres (funeral games for Aemilius Paulus), the audience left in search of a rumored gladiatorial combat. *Adelophoe* (*The Brothers*), which was given at the same games, was successful. *Phormio* and a third attempted and successful presentation of *The Mother-in-Law* were given at the Ludi Romani in 161 B.C. and 160 B.C. respectively.

The plays of Terence differed greatly from those of Plautus. Terence followed the simple style of Menander and Euripides. These models gave his plays a strong Hellenistic flavor—perhaps too much for the rough-and-ready Roman theatre audiences, who were unable to appreciate them fully. He was not a true man of the theatre, as Plautus was; literature had more appeal for him. His emphasis was on character portrayal, careful construction, and purity of idiom. His metrical system was much simpler than that of Plautus; his use of *cantica* was greatly reduced.[6]

NOTES

1. See Livy, *A History of Rome, Selections* (trans. and with an introduction by Moses Hadas and Joe P. Poe; New York: Modern Library No. 325, 1962), pp. 175–177.

2. See W. Beare, *The Roman Stage: A Short History of Latin Drama in the Time of the Republic* (3rd ed.; New York: Barnes & Noble, 1963), pp. 11–14, for a more complete account of Fescennine verses.

3. For an excellent treatment of the *fabulae Atellanae,* see Joel Trapido, "The Atellan Plays," *Educational Theatre Journal,* 18 (1966), 381–390, and also Beare, *op. cit.,* pp. 137–148.

4. Much pictorial material from Grecian vases concerning the *phlyakes* is presented in Margarete Bieber, *The History of the Greek and Roman Theater* (2nd ed. rev. and enlarged; Princeton, N.J.: Princeton University Press, 1961), pp. 129–146.

5. See Erich Segal, *Roman Laughter: The Comedy of Plautus* (Cambridge, Mass.: Harvard University Press, 1968), for an excellent account of Plautine comedy.

6. Consult Beare, *op. cit.,* pp. 45–78, 99–112; and George E. Duckworth, *The Nature of Roman Comedy: A Study in Popular Entertainment* (Princeton, N.J.: Princeton University Press, 1952), p. 501, for additional material on the works of Plautus and Terence.

5

$$\boxed{\text{ROMAN THEATRES}}$$

The Romans were unduly late in building permanent structures to house their theatrical performances. They waited until 55 B.C. before constructing a permanent stone theatre, well over 300 years after the first appearance of Etruscan dancers in Rome. One of the ironies of theatre history is that temporary wooden scene buildings in ancient Athens and portable wooden stages in Rome sufficed for the staging of plays during the most productive and creative theatrical periods of these two great civilizations. It appears that as more theatrical impedimenta are added, plays become less creative. It is true that pressures were exerted in Rome to erect more permanent theatre structures, but opposition was always too strong. Attempts were first made to build a permanent wooden theatre in Rome in 179 B.C. Although begun, it was never finished. Another was planned in 174 B.C. but never went past the planning stage. A third attempt was made in 154 B.C. with a stone theatre. This, however, was demolished by Senate decree before completion.

There are accounts, perhaps quite exaggerated, of at least three huge temporary wooden theatres that were built in Rome during the first half of the first century B.C. The one constructed by Claudius Pulcher in 99 B.C. supposedly had a stage wall (*scaenae frons*) so realistically painted to represent buildings that birds tried to perch on their painted brick roofs. The wooden theatre built by Marcus Aemilius Scaurus in 58 B.C. had an auditorium reputed to have held 80,000 people and a three-story stage: the lowest story was built of marble, the second of glass, and the third of gilded wood. The two large wooden theatres built by Gaius Scribonius Curio in 50 B.C., which were back to back, were used in the morning for plays, and in the afternoon could be turned around to form an amphitheatre for gladiatorial fights and other athletic contests.

At the same time, in southern Italy, especially in Sicily, there was no lack of Hellenistic theatres which were operating; it was a veritable beehive of theatrical activity. The area also had an abundance of portable wooden Greek *phlyake* stages. Roman colonists, once having escaped from direct control of their conservative Senate, even built a stone theatre (odeum) at Pompeii about 75 B.C., a mere five years after settling there.

PHLYAKE STAGES

Before conjecturing as to the configuration of early Roman portable wooden stages, one must examine the *phlyake* stages and a few features of Hellenistic theatres in Sicily. These were the closest models Livius Andronicus had to draw upon in creating stage facilities for his first productions in Rome in 240 B.C. *Phlyake*-type stages were probably adopted by Atellan-farce players and introduced into Rome before this time.

Current information on *phlyake* stages and staging methods is based on numerous vase paintings depicting *phlyake* scenes and stage settings from productions of the fifth and fourth centuries B.C.[1] Some vases discovered in various regions of southern Italy are generally believed to portray *phlyake* dramatic scenes, with which the vase painters took few liberties.

The scenes indicate that such stages were simple wooden affairs constructed for easy assembling and disassembling. The stages seemingly varied considerably in height. Some were fairly low and supported on rectangular posts. Others were provided with a series of five to seven steps leading from the ground to the center edge of the stage and facing the audience. Still others were even higher and supported by a series of columns. Many of these platform stages were provided with draperies, hung between the supporting posts or columns, which served as masking pieces. The rear stage walls were frequently provided with extra columns for decorative purposes. Doors were used often and windows occasionally to indicate an upper story. Infrequently a short sloping roof above the doors covered a tiny recessed vestibule area. *Phlyake* stages were small, shallow in depth, and narrow.

Phlyake vase painting of Cheiron the tutor climbing steps to what may be a small portable stage; he has the aid of his staff, a servant pushing him, and another servant pulling him by the head. The other figures are two old ladies conversing and a young male student of Cheiron's. (Courtesy, Trustees of the British Museum.)

Phlyake vase painting of Ares, wearing a plumed helmet, and Hephaestus fighting before Hera. The steps lead up to a stage. (Courtesy, Trustees of the British Museum.)

HELLENISTIC THEATRES OF SICILY AND POMPEII

A most vexing problem connected with attempts to reconstruct Roman portable wooden stages used for plays between 240 B.C. and 55 B.C. is that of stage width. Nearly all authorities agree that the stages accommodating these plays were extremely wide—wider than today's average stage in Broadway theatres. From a production standpoint, the internal evidence of the plays of Plautus and Terence supports this view. Later producers, coming after Livius Andronicus and before stone theatres were built in Rome, looked perhaps to the Hellenistic theatres of Sicily and the Hellenistic Theatre of Pompeii for wider and deeper stage models than *phlyake* ones. These were too small to serve adequately the needs of playwright-producers.

The Roman colonists' odeum at Pompeii had a stage 13 feet deep, 95 feet wide, and approximately 5 feet high—perhaps an ideal size for Roman plays. If these dimensions approached an ideal, then the Hellenistic theatres at Tyndaris, Segesta, and Pompeii furnished fine model stages. They were at least 90 feet wide, 10 or more feet in depth,[2] and equipped with a back-stage wall *(scaenae frons)* pierced by at least three *thyromata* capable of accommodating sturdy double doors so necessary for Roman comedy. Ramps or steps at either end of the wide stages facilitated entrances made by the actors from the sides. The main drawback in adopting these stages as models was their height. They were 8 feet or more above the orchestra level. However, a reduction in height from 8 feet to the 5 feet of later permanent stone theatres could easily have occurred in the course of 150 years. Finally, the horseshoe form of seating used in all Greek theatres probably carried over to the seating arrangements in the temporary wooden and later stone theatres of Rome.

TEMPORARY WOODEN THEATRES

In dealing with the controversies surrounding the temporary wooden theatres of Rome, scholars are confronted by three puzzling questions:

1. Where were these theatres placed in Rome when performances were given?
2. Were the spectators seated?
3. What were the stages and the stage buildings like?

Though the information is limited and often confusing, tentative conclusions are possible. Three locations have been suggested as likely spots for the temporary wooden theatres in Rome. These were the Forum, the circuses Maximus and Flaminius, and the open spaces in front of the Temple of Magna Mater, of Flora, and perhaps other temples. More positive information points to theatrical performances *(ludi scaenici)* being given in open spaces in front of temples rather than in any other single location.[3]

Whether the audience stood or sat in the temporary Roman theatres is subject to conflicting theories. Available evidence leans toward a seated audience.[4] This theory is based on a wall painting showing temporary wooden scaffolds used by Etruscan players, possibly in 364 B.C., to seat their Roman audience. Evidence from several prologues in the plays of Plautus refer to a seated audience, and also references within the plays, such as Lines 718–719 from *Aulularia* (*The Pot of Gold*):

> [*To audience*]   I pray your help.
> To point me out the man who stole the gold.
> Ay, there they sit in white like honest men.[5]

Finally, a number of references to seats in Roman theatres of the second century B.C. are contained in the works of Livy.

The following is conjectural material based on sufficient facts which warrant some reasonable assumptions.

The Plautine-Terentine theatres which served Roman theatre needs for more than 150 years, aside from perhaps the few notable exceptions mentioned earlier and until stone theatres were built, were temporary wooden platforms supported by legs or columns ranging in height from 5 to 8 feet, a minimum depth of 12 feet, and a width of at least 60 feet. Each platform was backed by a wooden wall *(scaenae frons)* at least 12 feet high and provided with three good solidly built double doors opening outward and slightly recessed. In all probability the *scaenae frons* was at first constructed simply. Later, it became more elaborate, with ornamental columns added and perhaps a window or two. Small, practical tile roofs may have jutted out from the top of the *scaenae frons.* In comedy, the stages represented a street or open place in front of a series of houses. In tragedy, they could represent a street in front of a palace or temple.

At either end of the stage were entrances/exits: the one on stage left supposedly led to the Forum and the center of the city; the one on stage right to the harbor and the country. Steps or inclined planes (ramps) similar to those used in several of the Hellenistic theatres bordered each end of the stages. Near one of the on-stage doors stood an altar, usually dedicated to Apollo,[6] although altars to other gods and goddesses were

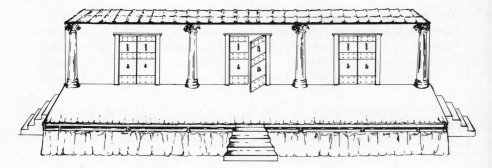

Reconstruction of a portable, wooden "Plautine-Terentine" stage. (Drawing by Martha Kaufman.)

often specified in the text of plays.[7] Props were brought in and left on stage throughout the performance or visibly removed as no front stage curtains existed to mask such operations until very late.

Short flights of steps led up to the stages from the orchestra, corresponding to those in *phlyake* theatres. The substructure of these stages was concealed by draped cloth hangings. The *cavea* (seating area) most likely consisted of a series of portable wooden scaffolds arranged in semicircular or horseshoe shapes following the Greek pattern with a short distance of space between the ends of the stages and the ends of the encircling scaffolds.

The Plautine-Terentine theatres must have been portable, capable of being assembled or taken down in a few hours' time and stored when they were not in use. But most important, these theatres were readily adaptable for staging the tragedies and comedies which were being written at that time. A play such as the *Miles Gloriosus* (*The Braggart Warrior*), produced at the Plebeian Games in Rome in 205 B.C., could easily have been staged in one of these theatres. The entire action of the play occurs on a street in Ephesus in front of the adjoining houses of Pyrgopolynices and Periplecomenus. The stage for this play would become the street, and two of the large adjacent double doors in the *scaenae frons* could serve as doors to the two adjoining houses. All the entrances and exits in the play are made from stage right, stage left, or from the two houses.

ODEA

Before considering the permanent stone theatres of Rome, it is necessary to make note of the stylistic architectural origins of these theatres, which are found in the early Roman odeum that evolved from the Greek odeion.

The odeion (Greek *ōidē* song) was a special building constructed for housing musical performances in ancient Greece. Later, it was copied, modified, and built throughout the Roman world. The odeum was provided with stone seats and a performing area which was, in most cases, a raised stage. Occasionally the buildings were covered with wooden roofs, and more often than not built in close proximity to large theatres. The odeion of Pericles, constructed about 446 B.C., adjoined a corner of the Theatre of Dionysus in Athens and is the oldest known example of this structural type. It was used as a rehearsal hall, a performance center for musical events, a meeting place, and a general-purpose auditorium. Also, the *proagōn* for the City Dionysia was held there. This odeion resembled the Thersilion (council house), the huge meeting building at Megalopolis and the Telesterion at Eleusis. According to Plutarch, it was a square "many-seated and many-columned" building.

The later Roman odea were rectangular auditoriums containing a raised stage area approximately 4–5 feet high, with semicircular rows of ascending seats for audience members. The Romans used their odea for both musical and dramatic performances. These structures were jointly influenced by Greek theatres and Hellenistic meeting buildings such as the Ecclesiasterion (assembly hall) at Priene and the Bouleuterion (council house) at Miletus. Within the latter was a huge rectangular building 114½ feet by 183 feet, of which slightly less than half was made into an odeum seating 1,500. For roofed-over odea, windows were provided in the upper parts for light.

Odea are found in many parts of Greece, North Africa, Turkey, and Italy. Wherever ancient theatres were located, odea were usually built nearby. The better-known ones are located at Corinth, Epidauros, Ephesus, Patras, Pergamum, Argos, Taormina, and Athens (Herodes Atticus). The best example is the small rectangular odeum at Pompeii, referred to above, which was built about 75 B.C. and had stone seats accommodating 1,500 spectators. At one time it was covered over with a wooden roof. This odeum is the oldest purely Roman theatre in existence, predating the Theatre of Pompey in Rome by 20 years, 48 years before Augustus became the first Roman emperor. Later Roman theatres closely followed its general pattern by:

1. Uniting the stage, stage house, orchestra area, and seating sections into one architectural unit and building it of stone situated on level ground.

2. Making orchestra and seating areas semicircular.

3. Building a low stage approximately 5 feet in height with a stage depth greater than that of Hellenistic theatres and very wide (95 feet for this theatre) surrounded on three sides by a decorative stage wall *(scaenae frons)* pierced at the back by three doorways and with another one at each side.

4. Creating vaulted side entrances to the lower seating sections of the theatre with special boxes *(tribunalia)* located above them.

5. Placing a few broad steps bordering the orchestra (four in this theatre) designed to accommodate movable seats for special honored guests. Often, this area was separated from the larger seating area directly behind by a stone parapet or barrier and a semicircular *praecinctio* (passageway). These barriers were later extended in height with reinforced metal fences to protect spectators when the theatres were used for baiting animals.

PERMANENT STONE THEATRES

Theatre construction in first-century B.C. Rome was linked to a general weakening of conservative forces strongly opposed to theatre. The wealthy and powerful of those affluent times wanted monuments to perpetuate their names and display their wealth.

Rome's first permanent stone theatre was built by Pompey in 55 B.C., during his second consulship. Forty-two years passed before the second was built, in 13 B.C., by L. Cornelius Balbus, the younger, which bore his name. Two years later, in 11 B.C., the last permanent theatre built in ancient Rome opened. It was built by Augustus as a memorial to his adoptive son Marcellus and dedicated in his name. The three theatres, if ever operated simultaneously, would have provided seats for 30,000 to 35,000 persons, a number considerably below the estimated seating capacity of the Roman Colosseum. Unfortunately, Rome's permanent theatres were not accompanied by a new creative surge. Literary dramas were on the wane and repertoires consisted principally of old plays, Atellan farces, mimes, and pantomimes.

THEATRE OF POMPEY[8]

Many details concerning the Theatre of Pompey are lacking; however, scholars are reasonably agreed on the following: It was located on level ground in the southern section of the Campus Martius, just west of the Circus Flaminius. Its estimated seating capacity has been placed between

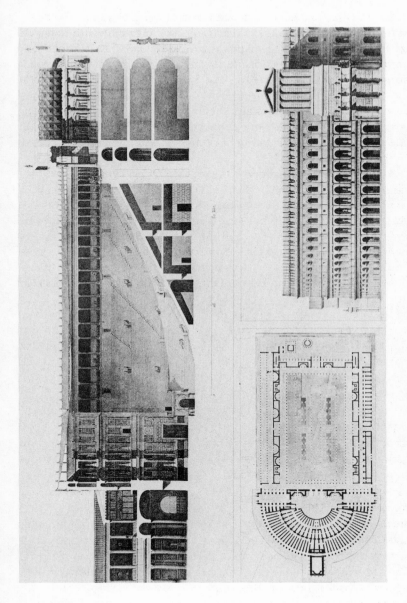

Ground plan and reconstruction of Theatre of Pompey, originally built in Rome in 55 B.C. (From D'Espouy, *Fragments d'Architecture Antique*, Vol. II [1901].)

8,000 and 10,000. The general ground plan of the theatre may be determined from the late Severian map (ca. 210 A.D.). However, the elaborate *scaenae frons* indicated in the map was probably added in one of many restorations and remodelings of the theatre's interior.

The orchestra was semicircular, and behind it was the semicircular auditorium. This consisted of three tiers of seats, separated by two *praecinctii* (passageways). Ascending stairs further divided seating into wedge-shaped sections. The auditorium connected with the stage house, thus creating a complete unit consisting of orchestra, scene house, and auditorium.

A covered colonnaded gallery at the top of the *cavea* (seating area) led right into the Temple of Venus Victrix. It was at the central portion of the *cavea* and extended beyond the auditorium. The temple, with rows of seats leading to it, made the entire building complex resemble one huge shrine honoring Venus. This scheme, according to Tertullian, helped allay Roman aversion to permanent theatre buildings, for under the temple steps were placed seats for spectators to watch the games. Technically, therefore, it was not a theatre. There is evidence that other shrines were located near the top of the *cavea*.

The theatre's exterior facade featured a series of arcades ornamented with columns. The lowest consisted of Doric columns, the second of Ionic, and the third Corinthian. Behind the scene house was the Pompeian Porticus, where spectators strolled before and during intermissions. It was a huge rectangular (590 feet by 435 feet) Hellenistic garden-park with colonnades.

THEATRE OF BALBUS

Except for the dedication date 13 B.C., its estimated seating capacity of 7,700, and its probable location in the Campus Martius, nothing more is known about the Theatre of Balbus.

THEATRE OF MARCELLUS

The lower two-thirds of the exterior facade of the Theatre of Marcellus still stands. The stage house, stage, *cavea*, and upper third of the exterior facade were destroyed when a series of palaces was built inside the theatre. This theatre was completed in 11 B.C. It seated approximately 14,000, making it the largest of the three permanent stone theatres. The reconstructed ground plan indicates that the vaulted side passageways between the stage *(pulpitum)* and the first tier of seats served as entranceways to the lower tier of seats. Above these were the *tribunalia,* reserved for those

Section of exterior of Theatre of Marcellus before restoration by Mussolini. The street-level arcades housed shops, while the upper levels were converted into palaces for wealthy Italians, destroying the stage and interior seating areas. (Photo Alinari.)

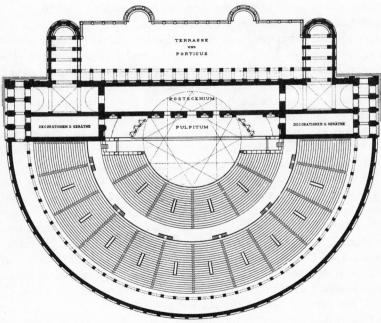

TERRASSE
UND
PORTICUS

POSTSCENIUM

DECORATIONEN U. GERÄTHE   PULPITUM   DECORATIONEN U. GERÄTHE

Ground plan of Theatre of Marcellus. (From Streit, *Das Theater* [1903].)

magistrates responsible for giving the *ludi scaenici*. Other seats in the theatre could be reached by the central passageway *(praecinctio)* and radiating stairways, or by stairways and tunnels under the seating areas opening into these areas by *vomitoria*. A colonnaded gallery was located at the top of the *cavea*. Storerooms on each side of the stage, a scene building directly behind the *scaenae frons*, and a rear terrace and portico completed this theatre complex.

The system of tunnels, stairways, *vomitoria*, colonnaded galleries, stage house, *pulpitum*, storerooms, and other features came into general use, with some variations, in the later Roman Empire theatres.

GRECO-ROMAN THEATRES

Once the Romans started their theatre-building program they were very busy constructing new theatres and remodeling and renovating Hellenistic theatres in the areas they were so rapidly acquiring. From all this activity two fairly distinct theatre styles emerged: the genuine Roman and the Greco-Roman. The genesis of the first style has been detailed. Later we will observe how it was codified by Vitruvius (ca. 16 B.C.) and followed in constructing the Empire theatres.

Greco-Roman theatres, however, blended stylistic features drawn in varying proportions from both Hellenistic and Roman theatres. There were remodeled Hellenistic theatres and new Greco-Roman theatres that adhered closely to the Roman style. Other renovated Hellenistic theatres made minor compromises and emerged with few Roman characteristics.

A fine example of a Hellenistic theatre almost totally converted into a Roman one was that originally built by Greek settlers in Pompeii about 200 B.C. This theatre underwent structural changes soon after the Romans moved into the area and built an adjoining odeum. By about 65 A.D. the following changes had been made: the ends of the scene building *(paraskenia)* were removed; the *parodoi* were vaulted and the *tribunalia* placed above them; three rows of wide steps for seating honored guests adjacent to the orchestra were installed; the stage was lowered; a decorative *scaenae frons* pierced by five doorways (one on each of the side ends, and three in the back) was constructed; two short flights of steps leading down from the stage to the orchestra were added; the *cavea* was enlarged; *vomitoria* were inserted; a covered corridor was built at the top of the *cavea;* and a *porticus* was created behind the scene building.

A Greco-Roman conversion of the Theatre of Dionysus, not quite as drastic as at Pompeii, occurred in 61 A.D., when Nero lowered that theatre's Hellenistic stage to about 5 feet and extended it forward into the orchestra. Backed by a two-story Roman colonnaded *scaenae frons,* its depth was 32 feet. The shrunken orchestra was paved with variously colored pieces of marble with a definite geometric pattern in the center portion. The orchestra was separated from the seating area by a marble barrier approximately 3 feet high. It became possible for Romans to bait animals and hold gladiatorial contests in this theatre. At the time of Phaedrus (ca. 270 A.D.) the stage (bema) was lowered further to 4 feet 9 inches and a set of stone steps leading down into the orchestra was added.[9] Changes wrought in the Theatre of Dionysus by Nero and Phaedrus are clearly evident in remaining ruins.

Greco-Roman theatres built in Turkey during the first and second centuries A.D. at Sagalassus and Termessus, among others, more closely resembled Roman theatres than Greek. However, stages for these theatres

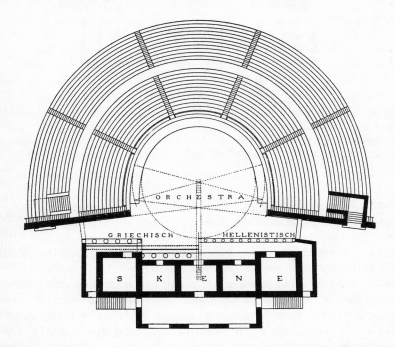

Ground plan of Theatre of Magnesia in Turkey showing how a 4th-cent. B.C. classical theatre, represented by section labeled *Griechisch* (Greek), was converted into a *Hellenistisch* (Hellenistic) theatre with a high, shallow, raised stage. A tunnel, called Charon's steps, was also added which led from the middle of the *skene* to the center of the orchestra. (From Dörpfeld and Reisch, *Griechische Theater* [1896].)

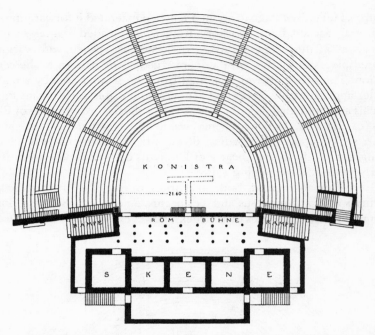

Ground plan of Theatre of Magnesia converted into a Greco-Roman theatre by extension of high Hellenistic stage farther into the *Konistra* (orchestra) to make a *Röm Buhne* (Roman stage). Ramps were added at each side of the stage, and a double set of steps was placed at the front, leading down to the orchestra area. (From Dörpfeld and Reisch, *Griechische Theater* [1896].)

were a compromise, retaining high Hellenistic stages deepened to conform to Roman patterns. At Sagalassus the stage was approximately 9 feet high and 24 feet deep, while that at Termessus was approximately 7½ feet high and 17 feet deep.[10] The front wall of the podium in both theatres contained a series of small doors leading below the stage. There, wild animals could be kept and released into the orchestra for animal hunts or baiting. Gladiatorial contests were also held in these theatres.

Many Greco-Roman theatres were originally Hellenistic theatres renovated as simply as possible to meet Roman staging requirements. This was accomplished in different ways. The same high stage may have been deepened by replacing the back stage wall and its *thyromata* with a new *scaenae frons* located several feet upstage of the old one. Alternatively, the high stage may have been deepened by a further extension into the orchestra. The former method was used at the Theatre of Oropus, of Sicyon, and of Priene where the stage was increased in depth from 9½ feet to 16½ feet. The latter method prevailed at the Theatre of Miletus and of Magnesia. At Ephesus, the stage was extended forward so as to give it a new depth of 20 feet, backed by a massive new towering *scaenae frons* 14 feet thick over-all replacing the old one.[11] Minor decorative architectural changes accompanied all of the above renovations.

THEATRES ACCORDING TO VITRUVIUS

Sometime between 16 and 13 B.C., Vitruvius' *De Architectura* (*Ten Books on Architecture*), containing important material on Greek and Roman theatres, made its appearance in Rome. Vitruvius Pollio was an architect, a profession whose members were responsible for designing and building theatres in Rome and in its provinces. He was writing at the time the Theatre of Balbus was under construction, some 40 years after the completion of the Theatre of Pompey. Vitruvius was obviously well acquainted with these two theatres and possibly knew something about the plans for the Theatre of Marcellus, which opened later, in 11 B.C. But he was not as well versed on Greek theatres as his book might indicate. Later Roman architects surely made generous use of his ideas in planning and laying out construction details for public buildings and theatres throughout the Empire.

The key Vitruvian concepts for planning a Roman theatre were these:[12] Plans for a theatre begin with a large circle. The diameter determines the size of the theatre, as all major measurements relate to it. Superimpose within it four equilateral triangles of the same size. The 12 points of the triangles touch the edge of the circle and are equidistant from each other, as indicated in the figure on p. 102. The base of the triangle (A-B), whose point G touches midway between the back of the last row of seats and the front row of seats bordering on the orchestra, forms the middle section of the *scaenae frons* of the scene building. The line C-D bisecting the circle marks the front of the stage *(pulpitum)*. Over-all stage depth will be half the radius of the circle. For example, if the circle were 80 feet in diameter, the stage would be 20 feet deep. The back wall of the stage building is marked by points L, K, and M, apex points for three of the triangles.

The stage should be no more than 5 feet high in order that spectators sitting in the orchestra may see the performers on the stage.

Points C, E, F, G, H, I, and D indicate where ascending stairs in the seating section *(cavea)* should be located for the lowest tier of seats. Stairs

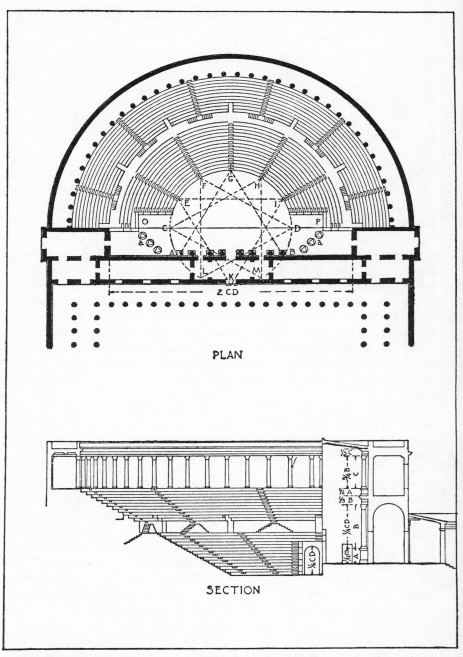

Ground plan and cross-section of a Roman theatre according to Vitruvius. (From
Vitruvius, *Ten Books of Architecture,* trans. by Morgan [1914].)

in the second tier of seats should be placed between those in lower sections.

The roofed colonnade built at the top of the last row of seats should be at the same level as the top of the scene building in order to improve acoustics.

Seats in the section O-P on both sides of the orchestra need to be cut away to allow for vaulted entrances. On top of these would be boxes *(tribunalia),* seats for officials sponsoring the plays.

The length of the *scaenae frons* should be twice the diameter of the orchestra. If the orchestra is 80 feet in diameter, the stage would be 160 feet wide, as indicated above.

The doorway opposite point K in the *scaenae frons* is the "royal door" *(aula regia),* and the doorways opposite L-M lead to guest chambers.

Other items indicated by Vitruvius were the revolving decorated triangular prisms *(periaktoi)* located in niches of the *scaenae frons* at stage right and left beyond the doors leading to the guest chambers. And beyond them are side entrances—"one from the Forum, the other from abroad." Descriptions are also given for the three scenes—tragic, comic, and satyric —which later had a strong effect on Italian Renaissance stage scenery.

None of the ruins of Empire theatres suggest that theatre architects followed precisely the proportional measurements outlined by Vitruvius or all of his specifications.

STONE THEATRES OF THE EMPIRE

Theatre and amphitheatre building outside of Rome gained momentum in the first and second centuries A.D. Emigration to the provinces greatly increased under Augustus and following emperors. Residents in Roman provinces were granted citizenship, further aiding the Romanization of North Africa, Spain, and Gaul. Eastward expansion of the Empire was also under way. Strong Hellenistic influences resulted in a blending of two cultures in Greece, its former colonies in western Turkey, and the entire Aegean area. Greco-Roman theatres, previously discussed, were a product of this process. From 98 A.D. to 180 A.D. a series of enlightened, cultured emperors, together with excellent administrators of the provinces and a long spell of prosperity and relative peace, greatly helped to solidify and encourage civic building throughout the Empire.

Excellent examples of Empire theatres are to be found in the ruins and partial restoration of theatres at Ostia, Minturno, Benevento, Verona, and Fiesole—all in Italy. Others are in southern France at Vaison, Lyon, Arles, and the well-preserved one at Orange from the Augustan period. In North Africa there are beautiful theatres at Sabratha, Timgad, Dugga, and Leptis Magna. The last-named was built about 2 A.D. Another well-preserved theatre, built between 161–180 A.D., is at Aspendos, Turkey.

Features common to many Empire theatres are to be found in the Theatre of Orange. It was a unified stone (limestone) structure located on flat ground with a semicircular *cavea,* once containing three tiers of seats topped by a colonnaded passageway.

A *porticus* directly behind and adjoining the scene building, constructed similar to the earlier Theatre of Pompey, was a feature shared by a few theatres. The *porticus* built directly behind the large theatre at Pompeii was probably created when it was converted into a Greco-Roman theatre. It was later used as a training school for gladiators.

The huge, highly decorative, three-story, colonnaded *scaenae frons* was once adorned by 76 large columns and numerous smaller ones, together with niches for statues. The large niche located directly above the central doorway contained a statue of the reigning emperor, designed so that the

Reconstruction of Theatre of Ostia after enlargement (ca. 200 A.D.); it was originally built early in the Empire period. The *scaenae frons* is elaborately decorated with columns and statues. (From D'Espouy, *Fragments d'Architecture Antique,* Vol. II [1901].)

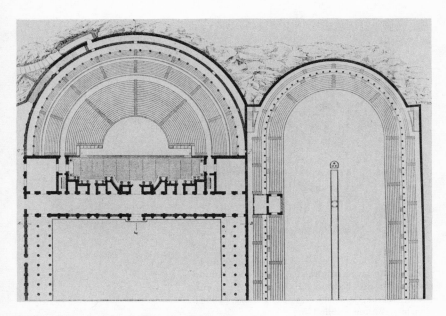

**Partial ground plan of Theatre of Orange and
adjacent circus.** (From Baumeister, *Denkmaler des
Klassischen Altertums,* Vol. III [1889].)

head could be replaced when a new emperor took office. A large doorway
in the center of the *scaenae frons* and two smaller ones bordering it, one
on each side, together with a doorway at each end of the stage leading into
the *paraskenia,* were provided. It should be noted that architectural ornamentation in Empire theatres varied greatly.

The wooden stage was 43 feet deep, 206 feet wide, and approximately
4 feet high. Above it an elaborately decorated wooden roof slanted up-
ward toward the stage front, thus improving acoustics and protecting the
scaenae frons from the weather.

The semicircular orchestra was 100 feet in diameter.

Stone corbels with holes for masts located on the upper part of the scene
building once supported awnings *(vela)* extending from the roof of the
colonnade atop the *cavea* to the back wall of the scene building. The *vela*
protected the spectators from the hot sun. It is thought that instead of
completely covering the top of the theatre, they were manipulated by
sailors so that they followed the path of the sun and so furnished shade
for audience comfort. On windy days the flapping of the *vela* was a great
distraction.

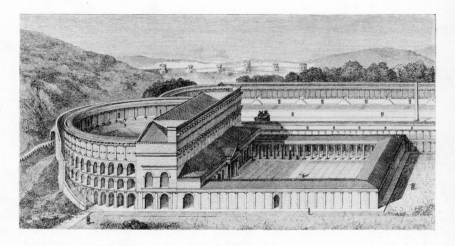

Reconstruction of Theatre of Orange showing its *porticus*, the large colonnaded court area behind the stage house; beyond the theatre is the circus. (From Caristie, *Monuments Antiques à Orange* [1856]. Courtesy, Boston Public Library.)

Reconstruction of Theatre of Orange showing *scaenae frons*, orchestra, and part of seating area. (From Caristie, *Monuments Antiques à Orange* [1856]. Courtesy, Boston Public Library.)

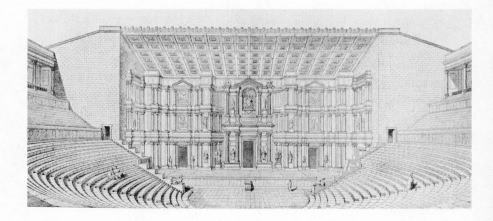

A front stage curtain *(aulaeum)* supported on a series of poles which traveled up and down in wood-lined stone slots was located just in front of the stage. Possibly the stage curtain rose to a height of 10 feet above the stage floor level.

ROMAN THEATRES IN RETROSPECT

The earliest Roman theatres consisted of portable wooden stages and bleachers patterned after *phlyake* stages of southern Italy and influenced in certain respects by Hellenistic theatres of Sicily. The odeum at Pompeii introduced architectural innovations into theatre construction to be followed in subsequent Roman theatres with variations, additional refinements, and improvements. The three permanent stone theatres built in Rome during the first century B.C. were enormous structures, elaborately decorated with columns, arches, religious shrines, and other ornamentation. When the Romans moved eastward and south into Grecian territory, theatre architects began blending Hellenistic and Roman patterns into a new Greco-Roman style. During the Empire period the Romans reached their peak in theatre building, creating huge stone theatres in key world centers under their control.

The stages of all the Roman theatres were at one time used for plays, Atellan farces, mimes, and pantomimes. Attention in the next chapter is focused on the production methods, the staging practices, used by the ancient Romans.

NOTES

1. Margarete Bieber, *The History of the Greek and Roman Theater* (2nd ed. rev. and enlarged; Princeton, N.J.: Princeton University Press, 1961), pp. 129–146. Also see W. Beare, *The Roman Stage: A Short History of Latin Drama in the Time of the Republic* (3rd ed.; New York: Barnes & Noble, 1963), pp. 335–339, for a discussion of "The So-Called 'Phlyax' Vase-Paintings of South Italy as Evidence for Staging."

2. The stage at the Theatre of Segesta was 11½ feet deep, and the Theatre of Syracuse was 13 feet deep, according to William Bell Dinsmoor, *The Architecture of Ancient Greece: An Account of Its Historic Development* (3rd. ed. rev.; London: B. T. Batsford, 1950), p. 303.

3. See John Arthur Hanson, *Roman Theater-Temples* (Princeton, N.J.: Princeton University Press, 1959), pp. 9–26; and Catherine Saunders, "The Site of Dramatic Performances at Rome in the Times of Plautus and Terence," *Transactions of the American Philological Association,* 44 (1913), 87–97.

4. Evidence supporting the contention of seated spectators in these theatres has been carefully sifted by Beare, *op. cit.,* pp. 171–172, 241–247.

5. From Plautus, *The Pot of Gold* (trans. by Sir Robert Allison), in *The Complete Roman Drama* (ed. and with an introduction by George E. Duckworth; New York: Random House, 1942), p. 149.

6. Apollo's altar is mentioned as being on the stage in *Aulularia, Bacchides, Mercator, Mostellaria,* and *Andria* according to Catherine Saunders, "Altars on the Roman Comic Stage," *Transactions of the American Philological Association,* 42 (1911), 96.

7. Altars to Diana, Lucira, and Venus are also mentioned as being on the stage in other Roman comedies. See George E. Duckworth, *The Nature of Roman Comedy: A Study in Popular Entertainment* (Princeton, N.J.: Princeton University Press, 1952), p. 83.

8. A very good account of the Theatre of Pompey is presented by Hanson, *op. cit.,* pp. 43–55.

9. For further details on the changes made by the Romans in the Theatre of Dionysus, consult Bieber, *op. cit.,* pp. 213–215, and Sir Arthur W. Pickard-Cambridge, *The Theatre of Dionysus in Athens* (Oxford: Clarendon Press, 1946), pp. 247–264.

10. Dinsmoor, *op. cit.,* p. 309.

11. *Ibid.,* p. 308.

12. This material summarizes the description given by Vitruvius for planning a Roman theatre as presented in his *Ten Books on Architecture* (trans. by Morris Hickey Morgan; New York: Dover Publications, 1960), pp. 146–150.

6

THEATRICAL PRODUCTION IN ROME

The vigor and vitality of the Roman theatre were hampered, thwarted, and perverted by various forces. From the beginning, Roman theatrical performances were joined to festivals crowded with a wide range of spectacular events which overshadowed and subordinated them. Consequently, Roman drama never rose to dominate festival activity as it had in Greece. Moreover, large segments of the early conservative Roman population were vigorously opposed to the theatre and would not support it during its struggle to establish roots. The strong Greek theatrical influence which poured in did not help matters, for it weakened native Roman theatrical creativity, especially that which affected literary drama. Most importantly, a drastic lack of freedom for playwrights to engage in open, meaningful dialogue on social and political issues of the day stagnated their drama for centuries and finally, with the increasing decadence of public taste, brought it to an inglorious end.

LUDI

The *ludi* in Rome were state religious games—festivals given to help expiate offenses against the gods, avert divine wrath and punishment, and win favor in general of the gods. The *ludi* included a wide assortment of events. There were chariot races, gladiatorial combats (most often given at special games), *venationes* featuring animal hunts or men fighting with animals, boxing and wrestling matches, specialty acts, sporting events, and theatrical performances. As the number of state games increased in the third and second centuries B.C., others were added to celebrate particular occasions, such as a military victory, a funeral, the dedication of an important building or temple. In earlier days occasional games were given in honor of Jupiter and Consus (deities associated with horses and mules) and were finally combined (ca. 366 B.C.) into the Ludi Romani and given annually September 4–19, the festival time span eventually reached in the Empire period. Theatrical performances *(ludi scaenici)* were added to this festival in 364 B.C. and 240 B.C., when a tragedy and comedy translated and adapted from the Greek by Livius Andronicus were presented.

Since *ludi* were open-air festivals lasting a number of consecutive days, they tended to cluster around the late spring, summer, and autumn months. The Ludi Plebeii (November 4–17) were begun about 220 B.C., with approximately three days allotted to theatre performances after 200 B.C. The Ludi Apollinares (July 6–13), instituted in 212 B.C., had two days given over to theatre performances by 169 B.C. The Ludi Megalenses (April 4–10) were started in 204 B.C., with theatre performances added in 194 B.C.; after 191 B.C. six days were occupied with theatre performances. The Ludi Cereales (April 12–19) commenced in 202 B.C., with two days for theatre performances; more were added later. The Ludi Florales (April 28–May 3) were made annual in 173 B.C., with the probability that mime performances were included at the start.[1]

LUDI SCAENICI

Once *ludi scaenici* were added to the games, they tended to occupy more and more days. For example, the Ludi Romani by 214 B.C. increased from one to four days, thereby making possible the production of as many as four to eight plays; by 70 B.C. 9 of the 15 days of the festival were occupied with theatre performances. It has been estimated that the Roman public was provided with 11 days of theatre performances in 200 B.C., and the number of days for this type of entertainment increased until during the reign of Augustus they reached a total of 43 days. In the late Empire (354 A.D.) as many as 100 of the festival days were given over to theatrical performances.

To these may be added private performances of pantomimes, plays, and readings from plays given for various societies and individuals to help celebrate births, marriages, and other events. However, the statistics for theatrical performances are highly suspect and not very meaningful, for we can be sure that a fine dividing line was not drawn to separate the types of *ludi* activity as neatly as many have been led to believe. Furthermore, the general decline and decadence of the Roman theatre was in full swing at the very time when great numbers of days were supposedly devoted to theatrical performances.

FINANCES FOR LUDI

All state *ludi* were held under the supervision of high magistrates; at first the consuls; afterwards and almost exclusively, the curule and plebeian aediles; and after Augustus, the praetors. Expenses came out of monies specially appropriated by the state for this purpose and turned over to the person in charge of the games. If this sum was insufficient, more was provided by presiding magistrates or by wealthy, public-spirited individuals. During the first century B.C. private expenditures for the games increased enormously, but not for the theatrical sections. Augustus and later emperors tried to check the mounting expenses and lavishness of the games, but without success. The public was always admitted free of charge to all games.

TRAGEDIES AND COMEDIES IN PRODUCTION

It must be kept in mind that the vast majority of Roman comedies and tragedies, most certainly the best ones, were originally written or translated to be produced in temporary, portable wooden theatres of the kind described in the last chapter, when literary drama was at its peak.

PRODUCERS

Livius Andronicus and Gnaeus Naevius each served as his own actor-manager *(dominus gregis).* They negotiated contracts, for payment to themselves and their companies, with the officials in charge of the *ludi scaenici;* organized their own acting companies; rehearsed and acted with the troupe; and saw to it that the plays were costumed and properly mounted. Other playwrights probably followed this practice down to the beginning of the second century B.C. When the number of *ludi scaenici* increased, management functions were taken over by leading actors, who served as actor-managers, much like those in nineteenth-century London.

Actor-managers purchased their play manuscripts from playwrights and retained all rights. Terence received 8,000 sesterces for *The Eunuch*, his most successful play. It was the highest sum paid for any comedy up to that time.[2] "The early dramatists must have owed much of their success" to the actor-managers.[3] There is good reason to believe that T. Publilius

Pellio, Rome's first full-time professional actor of whom we know anything, produced the plays of Plautus and played several of the leading roles. He must have been a fine actor, for his name was linked by Symmachus (a fourth-century A.D. orator and writer of letters) to Rome's best actors. The actor-manager Ambivius Turpio was responsible for producing Terence's six comedies and is credited with gaining an audience for the plays of Caecilius Statius as well as encouraging him in his work.

MANAGERS AND ACTORS

The status of the actor *(histrio)* in Roman society is difficult to determine. From the welter of controversy, the following might be deduced.[4] From 240 to about 200 B.C. playwrights acted in their own plays and recruited other actors wherever they could find them among Atellan-farce players and the ranks of semiprofessional actors. The latter were free citizens engaged in acting as a part-time occupation, for there were few opportunities to earn a full livelihood as actors. Conservative Romans looked with disfavor on acting as a profession. Acting troupes were kept small (five to seven members), and doubling in roles continued to be practiced as it had been in Greece.

From 200 to about 150 B.C. conditions of actors improved greatly. With actor-managers in charge of companies, the acting profession picked up momentum and many actors supplemented their incomes by playing in Atellan farces. Others, such as Pellio (actor-manager), Ambivius (actor-manager), Atilius (actor-manager), Minucius, and Cinius were able to devote full time to their profession. Acting finally reached its peak (150 to ca. 50 B.C.) as a profession with such actors as Roscius, Aesopus, Rupilius, Statilius, Panurgus, Eros (trained by Roscius), Spinther, Pamphilus, Antipho, and Diphilus, the last of the great tragic actors. Judging from such reports of their work as have come down to us, they were highly skilled, much admired for their vocal abilities and use of gestures, well paid, and free men.

Evidence is too slim to warrant the accusation that slaves were acting in Roman theatres at this time. Perhaps a few that were freed acted. Indications are that there was strong competition between acting companies and actors, that awards for excellence were given, and that all acting roles were filled by men. After about 50 B.C. and through the Empire period, acting in legitimate plays fell off drastically. Slaves entered and took over the acting profession.

The two great giants of Roman acting, Roscius and Aesopus, deserve special attention. If reports may be believed, Roscius ranks with the world's best actors and Aesopus was not far behind. For centuries the remark "He was a second Roscius" has been applied to great actors. Roscius was born about 130 B.C. By the time he was 45 years of age he had reached his acting peak, and in the course had acquired considerable wealth. His abilities earned him the friendship of Sulla, a Roman dictator who may have raised him to equestrian rank. He was also on intimate terms with Cicero, one of his great admirers who defended him in a lawsuit against a former acting pupil named Chaera.

The fame of Roscius as a teacher of acting has been well established. As an actor he was particularly noted for his "mellow voice, his ease of manner, the beauty of his person, his accuracy of expression and accent, which were the delight of Roman audiences."[5] These attributes served

Roman comic actors (3rd cent. B.C.) on cover of Praenestine Cista. (Courtesy, Trustees of the British Museum.)

him well in women's parts, parasites, and as a young leading man—all in comedies at which he excelled, although he acted in tragedies as well. He died in 62 B.C., a wealthy, respected man.

Aesopus (?–54 B.C.), who may have been Greek by birth, was at his best acting in tragedies. His performances were very convincing, and their realistic quality won the praise of Cicero. Once, according to Plutarch, he was so carried away in playing the part of Atreus that with his sword he killed a servant near him. Apparently his acting style lived up to the virile, robust quality needed to play Roman tragedies successfully. It also paid off at the box office, for when Aesopus died he left a large estate.

A favorite pastime of Roscius and Aesopus was to visit the Forum in order to study the art and artifices of noted orators. Evidently they were close friends with many of them and freely discussed and compared their arts. The writings of Quintilian are filled with comments on the similarities between acting and oratory.

Most of the actors from the Empire era—all of them slaves—whose names are known were Atellan-farce players, mime players, or pantomimists. Two of the best legitimate actors were Demetrius and Stratocles. Greeks by birth, they were highly praised by Quintilian for their acting skill. Juvenal commented on their excellence in feminine roles. Other actors of this period were Apelles, a favorite of Caligula; Glyco, who pleased Nero so much that he freed him; and the comic actor Actius, who was freed by Tiberius after pressure had been exerted by the actor's friends.

PRODUCTION AND ACTING STYLES

The description and reconstruction of comic acting style are more plausible than for tragic acting, since we possess a number of the comic plays. With respect to tragedy we can only speculate that Roman tragedy, with its rhetorical quality, vigorous style of writing, and many characters not too minutely depicted, favored a more formal type of acting—slightly artificial, highly declamatory, and accompanied by sweeping movements and gestures. The Empire added an enormous amount of spectacle in the staging of tragedies. Most likely a broader acting style developed to keep pace with the huge new stone theatres with their immense stages.

Roman comic acting was presentational, audience-oriented, vaudevillian, theatrical, and contrived. It was conditioned by loosely structured plays written to amuse and entertain an admission-free, restless, inattentive, outdoor audience.

Judging from the extant plays of Plautus and Terence, Roman comedies were peopled with stock characters. Among them were intriguing slaves, pimps, courtesans, bawds, long-lost daughters, bragging soldiers, parasites, cooks, shrewish wives, old men (bachelors or fathers), and irresponsible young men. The plots were also stock, revolving around deception, intrigue, trickery, and mistaken identity. The plays were filled with asides, soliloquies, direct address to the audience, eavesdropping, squeaking doors, and such comic fare as drunkenness, threats of beating, beatings, name-calling and verbal abuse, pretended dreams, and ever-ready knives of sadistic cooks. All this comic business and nonsense put a tremendous burden upon the actors, who had to be highly skilled performers.[6] Cicero paid them a high compliment when he said: "Everything is done by the stage player unexceptionally well: everything with the utmost grace: everything in such a way as is becoming and moves and delights all."

Roman comedies contained dances, featured *diuerbia* (spoken dialogue portions), and *cantica* (songs and sections of dialogue accompanied with Roman pipe music, some given no doubt in a recitative manner). Since *canticum* lines outnumbered *diuerbium* lines in most of the extant plays of Plautus and Terence and probably in other Roman comedies, comic actors had to handle songs, dances, and recitative parts, much as today's musical-comedy actors do. It is not reasonable to assume, as many have, that the *canticum* portions were sung by special singers brought onto the stage for this purpose or that an actor mimed while his counterpart sang for him.

MASKS

Masks were most likely used from the beginning in Roman comedies and tragedies and continued to be worn by all actors as long as these plays were given. Scholars with this viewpoint reinforce it thus:[7] First, all roles in Greek drama, except possibly for a few of them in the mimes, were played by masked actors. Therefore, the mask would hardly be omitted when this drama was translated into Latin and played in Rome. Second, frequent doubling in roles by actors, with scarcely time for elaborate changes in makeup and especially hairdos, was aided by using masks. Third, masks greatly facilitated the playing of women's roles by men. Fourth, comedies based on mistaken identity of twins or people who looked alike were very popular; masks solved this casting problem. It is also reputed by some that the mask was first introduced into the Roman theatre by Roscius in order to hide his squint.

Pictures of Roman tragic masks found in wall reliefs and marble and

Relief showing Roman comedy masks of father
and son, young man, and slave. (Vatican Museum.
Photo Alinari.)

Marble copies of Roman tragic masks of Hercules
and two bearded heroes (ca. 200 A.D.) found in
Theatre of Ostia, showing huge mouth openings,
large eye holes, and high *onkos.* (Photo Alinari.)

terra-cotta masks depict them with huge, exaggerated openings for the mouth, large holes for the eyes, abundant, curled hair on a very high *onkos* (forehead part), and full beards for men. The comedy masks appear to be less exaggerated, but still with large mouths. The Hellenistic masks described in detail by Pollux were carried over directly into the Roman theatre and served very effectively.

COSTUMES

Actors in the *fabulae palliatae* adopted Greek dress. The Ionic chiton (a rectangular piece of cloth draped around the body) served as the basic

Left: Marble statuette of Roman comedy running slave wearing fringed *palla* over his chiton and holding a mask. (Photo Alinari.) Right: Ivory statuette of Roman tragic actor showing high *onkos* and large eyes and mouth openings in the mask (ca. 2nd cent. A.D.). Thick-soled shoes may be concealed by the long robe. The pegs under the feet probably secured the statuette to a base. (From Baumeister, *Denkmaler des Klassischen Altertums*, Vol. III [1889].)

garment for male and female stage costumes. Male slaves wore it over padded, flesh-colored, Old Comedy tights. Younger men appeared in short chitons. The outer garment for a woman consisted of a himation *(pallium)* and for a man a *palla,* both of which were oblong pieces of cloth draped over the chiton in various ways. Comic actors wore sandals or slippers *(socci).* When a character needed to disguise himself, he placed a patch over one eye, donned a traveling hat and chlamys (an outer cloak which usually enveloped the left shoulder and part of the side of the wearer). Soldiers carried swords, cooks usually appeared with a large knife or some cooking utensil, old men were aided by walking staffs, and parasites were provided with oil flask and scraper. The color symbolism for New Comedy stage costumes was transported to Rome along with the play scripts.

In the *fabula togata* (comedy based on Roman materials) the actors wore Roman dress throughout; while in the *fabula praetexta* (historical play based on upper-class Roman life), the actors used the purple-striped toga of the magistrates.

Costumes for tragedies were taken *in toto* from the Greeks except that *cothurni* (Greek *kothornoi*) were made higher and the rich costumes were padded out more.

ATELLAN FARCES, MIMES, AND PANTOMIMES IN PRODUCTION

The shift from regular plays to the more popular Atellan farces, mimes, and pantomimes occurred in Rome during the first century B.C. and gained momentum during the Empire. The Silver Age, rich in many forms of literature, was totally lacking in quality drama. The common man, together with an increasing slave population, looked more and more to low-level amusement, as supplied by Atellan-farce players and mimes.

This lowering of theatrical tastes was tied directly to the increasing sensationalism of the arena. As always, theatrical producers, in order to remain in business and survive on a competitive basis, gave the public what it wished to see or thought it wished to see. Producers of regular plays countered with revivals of plays in the new stone theatres which were more noted for their scenic spectacle and performance virtuosity. Audiences for these performances came largely from an educated minority. The wealthy class, particularly its more sophisticated and jaded members, were enamored with the new flourishing pantomimes and tragic recitations.

ACTORS, COMPANIES, AND ACTING STYLES

Atellan-farce players were organized into companies who played together over long periods of time. The four stock characters had special requirements: Bucco was the foolish talker, the fool; Dossenus or Manducus, the hump-back, had a sharp, wicked tongue; Maccus was the stupid, rustic glutton; Pappus, the old man, had a wandering mind and was often the butt of humor. Each character wore a mask that made him readily identifiable to the audience. Performance was based around the *trica* (episode), a situational type of intrigue which was highly exaggerated, very funny, and often crude and obscene. The plays were short, vigorous, indelicate works performed most often as theatrical afterpieces. Improvisational at first, they were later put into literary form, which lasted for a short time before they reverted to their original state. The names of one, possibly two of the actors are known to us.

The Roman mime was a peculiar mixture of entertainment skills, plays, and variety acts. Chief among the skills, aside from acting, dancing, and acrobatics, was rope-walking, stilt-walking, juggling, sword-swallowing, fire-eating and fire-spitting, mind-reading, displays of magic, animals performing under the guidance of trainers (some dogs and other animals performed in plays); there were also numerous buffoons with their tricks and funny business. Improvised playlets, later partially or completely written down, were only part of a mime performance.

Companies were under the control and supervision of *archimimi*. A company included men and women and varied in size from an estimated 10 or 15 to 60 or more. An *archimimus* or *archimima* (female manager, such as Claudia Hermione) was often chief actor or actress supported by a second actor, the fool (*stupidus* alias *sannio*), whose clownlike behavior consisted of distorting and imitating the leading actor's work. Popular stock characters completed the company personnel: parasites, shrewish wives, old men, dancers, acrobats, specialty artists, and figures drawn from Greek and Roman life.

In the Republic, mimes were very popular as afterpieces and began to replace the Atellan farces. In the later Empire, they moved to the top spot of programs, usurping the place of tragedies and comedies. Variety acts were most likely given at the beginning of performances and also woven into the main portion at appropriate spots; the whole proceeding concluded with a dance.

Mimes could play almost anywhere—private homes, temporary theatres of the early Republic, or the stage of the later stone theatres. All that was needed was a platform or a cleared space and a few props.

Troupes traveled throughout the vast Roman Empire, drawing audiences wherever they played.

Names of people importantly associated with mimes were: Sorix, archmime and friend of Sulla; Decimus Laberius, actor and the first to give mimes a literary form; Publilius Syrus, actor and occasional author of mimes who amassed a huge fortune from his work; Favor, archmime who recreated the character of the Emperor Vespasian at his funeral games; Latimus, favorite of the Emperor Domitian and partner of the mime Thymele; and the famous mimes Dionysia, Cytheris, and Theodora (later the wife of the Emperor Justinian).

Pantomimists became the darlings among the Empire entertainers, pampered by emperors and empresses alike, and supported lavishly by the supersophisticated and decadent. Every wealthy household was a patron of the art and owned, if it could afford them, both male and female pantomimists. The craze became so great that individuals of means and social standing studied the art under the supervision of special teachers. Private performances supplemented public ones as the latter were not given often enough to satisfy demands.

Romans had a keen appreciation for a fine speaking voice, oratorical ability, and the art of gesture. These were the qualities, as noted earlier, that brought fame and fortune to Roscius and Aesopus. Pantomime was a further extension of the art of gesture, carrying it into the realm of interpretative dancing which the Romans felt required the greatest skill. It was especially welcomed since so many different peoples were in the capital; it became a universal language understood by all, particularly by those acquainted with mythology and Greek tragedies.

Pantomimes were performed by single artists, most often men (there were women in the later Empire period) who danced several successive roles, changing masks and costumes as they proceeded with various male or female parts. They were accompanied by one singer or a chorus that sang the text, and a flute player or full orchestra of lyres, Pan's pipes, citharae, cymbals, and flutes, while a scabellum (foot-clapper) beat out the rhythm. The "book" or story was derived from Greek mythology, primarily but not exclusively from love stories. Costume and mask changes were covered by musical bridges, songs, or recitative.

Great skill was required when the pantomimist had to dance successively the roles of Bacchus, Cadmus, Pentheus, and Agave in a libretto composed by Statius, and, at the same time, suggest the whole story and the relationship of each character to the others. He needed a thorough knowledge and understanding of Greek mythology; he had to be good-looking, well-built, with a graceful body superbly trained and conditioned. Above all, he needed to convey a sense of refined sensuality, the

Ivory relief of female pantomimist holding three
masks (ca. 4th cent. A.D.). (Courtesy, State Museum
of Berlin.)

highpoint in most pantomimic performances. The principal offshoots of
strictly mythological pantomimes were the danced poems of Ovid and
panegyrics on emperors that were sung and danced.

The fame of pantomime artists, their support by important people, and
the popularity of the art itself have been documented to a degree.

The cofounders of Roman pantomime were Bathyllus, an Alexandrian
exponent of comic pantomime (a lascivious burlesque of the choicer
Greek myths), and Pylades, a Cilician supporter of tragic pantomime. The
latter was most successful as Bacchus and Hercules Furens, two of his best
roles. Both men started schools for training pantomimists. Later followers
evidently assumed their names. Pylades even wrote a book on the subject

of pantomime. He retired an extremely wealthy man.

Other famous pantomime artists were Hylas, a pupil of Pylades who often competed with him in public dancing contests. The name Paris was taken by at least three pantomimists living at different times, all renowned; two were involved in political intrigues, common for these artists because they were sometimes too close to the fountainhead of power and thereby constantly in danger of banishment. Menester was reputed to have been extremely beautiful, talented, a favorite of Caligula, and an unwilling lover of Claudius' wife Messalina.

MASKS AND COSTUMES

Atellan-farce players appeared in the dress of farmers and tradespeople. They went barefoot or wore the low comedy shoes *(socci)*. Their masks were slightly exaggerated and stylized to fit the intended character.

Front and back views of metal statuette of dancing, barefoot, female mime (ca. 200 A.D.) wearing *centunculus* with bells and cone-shaped fool's cap; she has clappers in her hands and a foot-clapper *(scabellum)* under her left foot. (A. M. Friend Collection. Courtesy, Art Museum, Princeton University.)

Pantomimic actors dressed in rich, specially designed costumes suitable for various roles. They changed their masks, provided with closed mouths in contrast to those worn in other forms of theatre, as they performed first one then another character.

The dress worn by mimes was as varied as their entertainment. Available information is sparse. The comic fool *(sannio)* wore a long, pointed, cone-shaped hat and a *centunculus,* a garment of colored patches similar to the later Harlequin costume. A few actors were equipped with the phallus and several may have worn masks; for the most part they were unmasked. This afforded them free play for facial expressions, so much enjoyed by the audiences. All went barefoot. This gave them greater agility, a distinct asset to many performers.

STAGE SCENERY AND MACHINERY

In viewing Roman theatre from modern times, it is important not to project into it current scenic conventions and stage devices. Roman stages, temporary and permanent, were always architectural entities basically identical for each play or theatrical work. Stage scenery (except for that which might have been displayed on the *periaktoi* located in niches in the *scaenae frons* on each side of the stage, for when revolved they showed their "three decorated faces") was built into the theatres and could not be changed. Props, such as altars, furniture, and so forth, could be added; curtains *(siparia)* could be hung here and there, but this was the limited extent of "set" alterations. Playwrights overcame this limitation by writing dialogue that set the scene for actors and audience alike. The *scaenae frons* was usually pierced by three doorway openings in the back, each provided with large, rugged double doors opening outward to the stage. These represented houses for the principal characters in comedies, a temple or palace for tragedies. The setting could be similarly interpreted for other forms of theatre (mimes, pantomimes, and Atellan farces) or could be just a platform for various acts. A doorway opening on each side of the stage in permanent stone theatres enabled actors to make entrances from the "wings" of the stage. Ramps or steps on each side of the stage served the same purpose in temporary wooden theatres.

The *scaenae frons* in the temporary wooden theatres was quite plain at first but probably became more elaborate; in the later stone theatres it was huge, gorgeously painted, columned, and decorated. The stages in both types of theatres may have been provided with at least one trapdoor (Charon's steps) for ghostly appearances. Thunder was produced by pour-

Large theatre at Pompeii showing trench for curtain and stone slots for curtain poles. (Photo Alinari.)

ing large stones from a jug into a brass jar. A mechanism for simulating lightning was used.

In 56 B.C., Cicero mentioned the front stage curtain *(aulaeum)* as being in operation. Ovid, Horace, Virgil, and Phaedrus all refer to it in some way.[8] The consensus holds that it was raised to conceal the stage (probably only its lower half or enough to hide the actors and stage props), was lowered to reveal the stage set at the beginning of a show, and was raised again at the end. The 56 B.C. date would indicate that the *aulaeum* made its appearance in Rome prior to the opening of the Theatre of Pompey in 55 B.C. How it was accomplished in a temporary wooden theatre is hard to understand. The Roman stone theatre at Arles, built about 46 B.C., has a row of stone slots obviously used for the up-and-down movement of front curtain poles. This, or a similar scheme, may have been introduced into several of the temporary Roman theatres in a modified form. An *aulaeum* may have been used even earlier (ca. 75 B.C.) in the large theatre at Pompeii, where stone slots for curtain poles and a trench for the curtain to rest in when it was lowered were provided. Several Roman theatre ruins besides that at Pompeii, including those at Syracuse, Arles, Orange, Fiesole, Lyon, Vaison, Timgad, and Dugga, are provided with *aulaea* trenches.[9]

AUDIENCES: REPUBLIC AND EMPIRE

As pointed out, Roman literary dramas or regular plays were Grecian, translated and adapted into Latin—a direct result of Roman soldiers being exposed to Greek plays during the First Punic War. The impact of these plays on stern, hard-working Romans of the mid-third century B.C. is debatable. No doubt, their appeal was limited at first. Audiences may well have been wary of this Greek innovation often witnessed for the first time. Then, before they could become popular, Hannibal invaded Italy and the new theatre was hit hard. The defeat of Hannibal in 202 B.C. cleared the way for the "philhellenism movement" started during the war when Greece asked for help to prevent Macedonia from springing to the aid of the Carthaginians. Cato's opposition to "literary theatre" did not defer its strongest period when the best of plays were written, to be followed by a period in which great actors dominated the Roman stage (150 to about 50 B.C.).

Better theatre audiences should have paralleled the rising dramatic and creative surge. This was not the case. They were a noisy, restless, boisterous, rude lot, more often interested in *who* was present *in* the theatre than in *what* was happening *on* the stage. Often, they were extremely volatile, ready to leave the theatre instantly when something more exciting was reported to be happening at another place. Many prologues, particularly those of Terence, contain pleas to the audience for attention. The endless repetitions in several comedies were undoubtedly dramatic devices to insure that inattentive audiences could follow the play's action.

Plays were given in the early afternoon. The only reserved seats during the Republic were those provided for senators after 194 B.C. This must have meant a mad scramble for good seats. All classes went to the theatre —men, women, children, and slaves. It was free to all, part of a holiday festival. Claques (hired applauders) were introduced by actor-manager-playwrights to gain audience support and convince those in charge of the festival of their work's merit. If successful, playwrights and actors were in a better position to increase their fees. Later, when claques for actors, mimes, and pantomimists appeared, they were a nuisance and on occasion became a menace.

During the second century B.C., as a result of the wars, the slave population began increasing at a terrific rate. Thousands of captives were brought back to Rome, a social upheaval directly reflected in Roman theatre audiences. The audience steadily declined in quality, especially when a stable middle class was replaced by *nouveau riche* leaders seeking amusement along with slaves at the bottom of the social ladder. By Cicero's time (106–43 B.C.) theatre-audience standards for entertainment had slipped greatly. Quality entertainment was no longer a major concern. Gladiatorial combats and wild-beast hunts held much more appeal. However, when popular star actors performed—Roscius, Aesopus, and others —they drew large crowds. As drama waned, the art of acting helped to preserve an interest in the theatre.

The early Empire era was devoted to revivals of comedies and tragedies mounted as spectacles with hundreds of extras. Eventually they were discontinued. Atellan farces were on the decline; mimes dominated the stage; pantomimes grew in popularity with the wealthy classes, and so did tragic recitations.

From the fourth century A.D. to about the end of the sixth century A.D. the Roman theatre was under almost constant attack from the Christian church, and to a lesser degree from the barbaric invasions from the north. The theatre also suffered as a result of its own excesses by catering to the jaded tastes of its audiences. As audiences degenerated, so did the theatre. Decadence, grossness, and increasing vulgarity marked most of the late Empire theatre. As Rome went into decline, its theatre followed.

NOTES

1. See George E. Duckworth, *The Nature of Roman Comedy: A Study in Popular Entertainment* (Princeton, N.J.: Princeton University Press, 1952), pp. 76–79; and Warde W. Fowler, *The Roman Festivals of the Period of the Republic: An Introduction to the Study of the Religion of the Romans* (London: Macmillan, 1925).

2. For additional material on the organization of the Roman theatre, see W. Beare, *The Roman Stage: A Short History of Latin Drama in the Time of the Republic* (3rd ed.; New York: Barnes & Noble, 1963), pp. 164–170.

3. Frank Tenney, "On T. Publilius Pellio, the Plautine Actor," *American Journal of Philology*, 53 (1932), 248.

4. Consult these works regarding the status of the Roman actor: Beare, *op. cit.*, pp. 166–167; Frank Tenney, "The Status of Actors at Rome," *Classical Philology*, 26 (1931), 11–20; Duckworth, *op. cit.*, pp. 75–76; and Kenneth G. Henry, "Roman Actors," *Studies in Philology*, 16 (1919), 334–382.

5. Henry, *op. cit.*, p. 351.

6. James H. Butler, "Roman Comedy," *Players Magazine*, 29 (1952), 28–29, 39.

7. The strongest cases for the use of masks in the acting of Roman literary drama from the time of its introduction into Rome are presented by A. S. F. Gow, "On the Use of Masks in Roman Comedy," *Journal of Roman Studies*, 2 (1912), 65–77; and Beare, *op. cit.*, pp. 192–194, 303–309.

8. Beare, *op. cit.*, p. 268.

9. Margarete Bieber, *The History of the Greek and Roman Theater* (2nd ed. rev. and enlarged; Princeton, N. J.: Princeton University Press, 1961), pp. 179–180.

7

GAMES AND SPECTACLES IN ROME

No treatment of theatrical matters in ancient Rome and its later ever-increasing empire would be complete without some attention to circus games *(ludi circenses)*; gladiatorial games *(munera)*, and the amphitheatres built to exhibit them; animal hunts and beast-baiting *(venationes)*; and ship battles *(naumachiae)* fought by armed gladiators, condemned criminals, or prisoners of war. These spectacular shows were paratheatrical in nature, filled with suspense, and often employed scenery, costumes, and some form of personation.

They had great drawing power among the Roman masses and were in open competition with the theatre *(ludi scaenici).* As they increased in popularity, they became more spectacular, brutal, and sadistic. Wherever the Roman legions and colonists spread out over Europe, Asia, and Africa, they took their various forms of entertainment with them, as the ruins today give silent testimony. The Romans remodeled Greek theatres and adapted them as makeshift amphitheatres or miniature naumachiae.[1] The orchestra area of the Theatre of Dionysus was converted into a watertight basin by the Romans sometime in the third century A.D.; and new, huge amphitheatres and circuses were constructed to accommodate their games and spectacles.[2]

Roman games grew out of religious observances, although the religious implications in some of them appear a little obscure to us and were perhaps less than obvious even to the Romans. In the later days of the Republic, helping to sponsor the games became a means whereby a wealthy person might purchase popular favor with the public. In the Empire period they became a form of narcotic, ready means of keeping the *populus* (common people) contented.

Bread and games *(panem et circenses),* in the words of Juvenal, were regarded as rights and all the new governments and emperors supported them, some with more fervor than others. But even those emperors who did not favor them, such as Nerva, Marcus Aurelius, and Antoninus Pius, were in regular attendance. Tiberius, reigning in the early days of the Empire, was the only Roman emperor to have spurned them completely, at least in the latter part of his rule. Friedländer has pointed out that the games served the emperors as excellent occasions for exposing themselves to "the assembled people" to learn their desires and wishes.[3]

CIRCUSES

The oldest games of Rome, and long the most popular, were those given in the circus. Included were horseraces featuring trick-riding, prizefighting of a very vicious nature, wrestling, foot-races, acrobatics, mock cavalry battles, exhibitions of wild and trained animals, baiting of wild animals, and the main feature—chariot races. The latter was one of the earliest forms of entertainment to reach Rome and soon became extremely dangerous, bloody, and exciting.

The first Roman circus (Circus Maximus) was introduced by one of the seven early kings, Lucius Tarquinius Priscus (616–578 B.C.), sometime in the late seventh or early sixth century B.C. and was located in a valley (Vallis Murcia) in Rome between the Aventine and Palatine Hills. The pattern adopted for the physical layout, the housing for this circus, was based on the Greek hippodrome (*hippos* horse, *dromos* course or road). It was introduced into Rome by way of the Etruscans. In later years Roman circuses differed markedly from the hippodrome of the earlier Greeks. There were eventually three circuses within the city of Rome and one (Circus Maxentius) three miles outside on the famous Appian Way. These were the Circus Maximus (ca. sixth century B.C.), the Circus Flaminius (221 B.C.), the Circus Neronis (erected by Caligula ca. first century A.D.), and the Circus Maxentius (309 A.D.).

Roman circuses were laid out on long, narrow stretches of ground. The Circus Maximus, the largest of all, was 2,000 feet long and 650 feet wide. This huge oblong space was surrounded by a podium, or raised platform, for seating high officials and by three tiers of seats located above it and separated by passageways which extended down the two long sides and

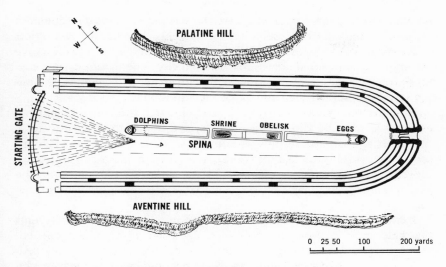

Ground plan of Circus Maximus. (Drawing by Martha Kaufman.)

around the semicircular or closed end. In the middle of this closed end was the triumphal gateway; it was later replaced by three arches through which the beginning procession for the games entered and the winners left. The earliest seats and other parts of the Circus Maximus were built of wood; eventually, in subsequent rebuildings, they were replaced with stone and marble. A moat several feet wide was at first built around the arena to protect the spectators from the wild animals used in the games. This was soon replaced by more practical iron grillwork.

The arena (sandy place) was covered by sand, as its name indicates, to protect the unshod feet of the horses. Down the middle of the arena for two-thirds of its length was a barrier *(spina)* set at a slightly oblique angle in order to give the chariots more room at the starting end. It separated the outward course from the return one. Three conical pillars *(metae)* were located at each end. In between were obelisks, images, statues, seven figures of dolphins near one end and seven oval eggs near the other; one of each was taken down to inform the spectators of the progress of the race as the charioteers made their rounds of the *spina.* Several rounds or laps constituted a race *(missus).* The twelve starting gates —wooden barriers *(carceres)* quite similar in principle to those used in modern horseracing tracks—were located at the opposite end from the triumphal gateway. Above the middle portion of the *carceres* was the box for the presiding magistrate who gave the starting signals. At each end of the *carceres* were towers resembling battlements, matched by two others at the corners of the closed end of the arena. From the outside they gave the appearance of the defenses for a walled city. The exterior, later covered with marble, was three stories high with arches and columns decorating it and resembled the exterior of the Colosseum.

Roman circuses accommodated several thousand spectators. It has been established that the Circus Maxentius seated about 25,000; the Circus Flaminius and Circus Neronis were much smaller. The Circus Maximus seated about 60,000 at the time of Augustus, but kept increasing its seating capacity with later renovations and by the time of Constantine, in the fourth century A.D., may have accommodated as many as 200,000 spectators.

Excitement, suspense, and the gambling instinct were the ingredients that held sway in the circuses. Several days before the games opened, astrologers were consulted, bets were placed, and magic was employed. Excitement reached a crescendo the day of the opening, as throngs of men and women made their way to the circus in the early hours before dawn. Special seats were provided for knights and senators; the general public scrambled for places, men and women sitting together—for many of the women were as addicted to chariot races as the men.

Games were officially opened with great pageantry. A huge religious procession *(pompa circensis)* started at the Capitol, passed through the triumphal gateway of the circus, and traveled the full length of the racecourse and around the *spina*. The praetor or consul giving the games, dressed as a triumphant general and surrounded by his family, stood in a chariot leading the parade preceded by a group of musicians—trumpeters and flute players. The lead chariot was followed by a gorgeous parade of litter-borne floats and carts drawn by mules on which rested statues and images of the gods and symbols and attributes of the priesthood. During the Empire period images of deceased, deified emperors with their empresses were included in the procession.

Immediately following the procession the seven-lap chariot races began. As many as 12 chariots could race at one time. The usual number was 4, although 8 was also common. The number of races held in one day varied from 10 or 12 to as many as 20 or 24. Teams of horses pulling the racing chariots consisted of 2, 3 (seldom), or 4 horses. Occasionally, 6 or as many as 10 horses would be used for special races.

Very soon chariot racing came under the control of four highly competitive companies or factions represented by the colors white, red, green, and blue, worn by their respective charioteers. Factions encouraged parti-

Reconstruction of Circus of Nero. (From Drum, *Handbuch der Architektur* [1905].)

sanship and heavy betting. Certain of the emperors were avid supporters of the blue and green factions. Nero once had the arena sand dyed green. At times, this obsession for factions gripped all of Rome in a tight vise, precluding and usurping other important business, cultural, and intellectual pursuits. The circus stirred the rivalries and passions of the Roman mob to an almost unbelievable pitch and ultimately helped to undermine the moral and social fabric of the Empire. Chariot racing was one of the few activities that outlasted the western Roman Empire and did not entirely vanish until the latter half of the sixth century A.D.

Charioteering was a dangerous, hazardous, and not very respectable occupation that drew its recruits from the lower classes, freedmen and slaves. The monetary rewards for charioteers were sizable, and numerous statues attest to their popularity. Collisions and accidents were common, and drivers smeared themselves with boar's dung hoping this might save them from massive infection if they collided or were mangled on the racecourse. The sharp turns around the ends of the *spina* were the most critical and accident-prone moments, and collisions at these points often proved fatal for drivers.

Terra-cotta plaque of charioteer about to round one end of the *spina*. (Courtesy, Trustees of the British Museum.)

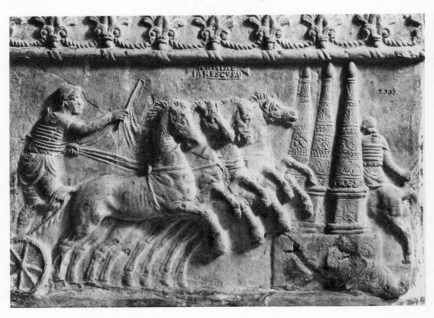

AMPHITHEATRES[4]

Some of the most dazzling, gruesome, and exotic spectacles staged in the ancient world took place in the Roman amphitheatres. These were free-standing, oval-shaped structures completely surrounding a central arena. Amphitheatres owed their birth to the development of gladiatorial games which originated in Etruria as part of the funeral games honoring dead heroes. It was thought that the blood of the vanquished gladiator falling on the ground would help to comfort and revive the spirits of the dead one. Gladiatorial combats were also popular in Campania, where specially trained slaves fought to the death in order to entertain guests at banquets. These contests made their way to Rome where it took them considerable time to gain in popularity. The first occurred in Rome in 264 B.C. when two brothers, Marcus and Decimus Pera, exhibited three duels between gladiators at their father's funeral. Exhibitions such as these occurred only occasionally during the early days of the Republic and were then private.

Before entering into a discussion of gladiatorial contests, it is necessary to examine the Roman amphitheatres developed to house them. The area surrounding the graves of dead heroes, the Forum with its hastily constructed wooden spectator stands, and the circus with its ever-present *spina* were poor places in which to hold gladiatorial contests.

To the Campanians goes the credit for building the oldest surviving amphitheatre (*amphi-* around, *theatron* viewing place) about 70 B.C., in Pompeii. This is one of the simpler amphitheatres, for it lacks underground structures or apparatus beneath the arena. Thus, it is similar to later amphitheatres at Arles and Nimes in France and at Verona in Italy. The arena for the Pompeian amphitheatre is sunk several feet below ground level—similar to the huge coliseum in Los Angeles, California— thereby saving the expense of constructing a lofty superstructure. The stone amphitheatre, 445 feet long by 341 feet wide, seated approximately 20,000 spectators. Those in the upper tier of seats entered by means of outside stairways; those in the lower two tiers entered vaulted passageways that led around and under the second tier of seats and out into a central passageway that circles the amphitheatre separating the first and second tiers of seats.

According to limited available source material, Rome may have had three amphitheatres before the Flavian Amphitheatre, later called the Colosseum because of the colossal statue of Nero which stood close to it, was completed during the reign of the Emperor Vespasian in 80 A.D.

These were a temporary wooden one built by Julius Caesar in 46 B.C., another built partially of stone by Statilius Tauraus in 29 B.C., and a third wooden one erected by Nero sometime during his reign (54–68 A.D.).

THE COLOSSEUM

The Colosseum belongs to the very advanced group of Roman amphitheatres that featured elaborate underground structures beneath the arena for the temporary housing of animals and for scenery used in various spectacles. A system for occasionally flooding the floor of the arena was provided. The arena was completely covered with movable flooring that permitted sections to be removed when needed. This flexibility enhanced the amphitheatre's general usefulness and made it possible to exhibit wild and rare animals with appropriate scenic decor and to stage *venationes,* which featured animal hunts and humans *(bestiarii)* fighting with animals. The latter required appropriate and colorful costumes as well as proper scenery. The scenic units, often very elaborate, as well as the animal cages could be hoisted from the underground level to the floor of the arena when needed. Flooding the floor of the Colosseum for crocodile and alligator hunts and for naumachiae (ship battles) was also possible.

Gladiatorial contests were easiest to stage and far outnumbered the other events held in the Colosseum. The amphitheatre at Capua, a leading gladiatorial contest and training center, and at Pozzuoli a few miles below Naples are both excellent examples of Roman building and engineering skills. The floors of these arenas and their complicated underground structures are in a relatively good state of preservation, but the seating areas have been almost completely destroyed.

The Colosseum was located near the civic center of ancient Rome, easily accessible to all. Its appearance today differs markedly from its once magnificent splendor. Several renovations and additions, plus the ravages of time, earthquakes, lightning, fires, and vandalism have reduced it to a mere carcass. For centuries it served as a marble quarry, furnishing building materials for numerous Roman churches. Nevertheless, it is still an imposing monument. Originally three stories high (120 feet), a fourth story was added sometime in the first half of the third century A.D., making it 157 feet tall with an over-all length of 620 feet and a width of 513 feet. The arena was 287 feet by 180 feet with an understructure going

View of ruins of Colosseum. (Photo Alinari.)

down 20 feet below it. Between 50,000 and 55,000 spectators were distributed among the four seating areas:

1. The podium was the choice area in the Colosseum. It was an encircling marble platform that skirted the arena 15 feet above the arena floor; 12 feet in width, it was protected from wild animals in the arena by a metal screen. On the podium were located the emperor's canopied throne, resting on a small tribunal (platform for magistrates), and special chairs for dignitaries.

2. Behind the podium a wide passageway completely encircled the Colosseum; above it were 20 rows of seats largely reserved for those of equestrian rank.

3. Above this, on the second tier of seats and separated from the first tier by a rounded corridor *(praecinctio)* and a low wall, were seats for the well-to-do Romans.

4. The third tier of seats and possibly a fourth one belonging to the third century A.D. were separated from those below by a high wall and were used by women, plebeians, and slaves. An ingenious system of stairways and vaulted passages was provided, designed to conserve

space while giving quick and easy access to all sections of the amphi-theatre.

An assortment of building materials—wood, concrete, brick, tufa, pum-ice-stone, travertine, and marble—was used in constructing the Colos-seum. The external facade, or outer wall, was divided into four stories. The first three consisted of a series of 80 open arcades for each level separated by three-quarter detached columns: Doric order for the ground level, Ionic order for the second level, and Corinthian order for the third. The fourth level was pierced by small windows. At the very top 240 stone corbels once held masts from which ropes were strung to support the movable *vela* or *velaria* (awnings) that protected the spectators from the hot Italian sun.[5] Many ancient writers mention devices to spray the air with water to cool and perfume it. Entrance to the Colosseum was gained through the lower 80 arches; the four at each end of the axis were the main entrances.

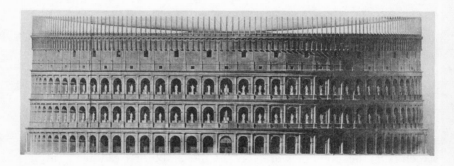

Exterior and interior reconstruction of Colosseum (3rd cent. A.D.) showing masts which supported the *velaria*. (From D'Espouy, *Fragments d'Architecture Antique* [1901].)

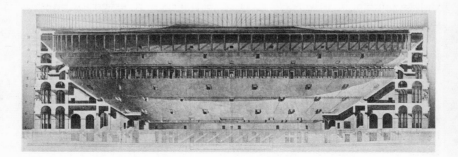

GLADIATORIAL GAMES

As mentioned earlier, gladiatorial games, following their introduction in 264 B.C., were fairly slow in developing in Rome and were held only occasionally in connection with the funerals of prominent wealthy men. It was not until about the middle of the second century B.C. that they began to increase in frequency and in numbers of gladiators involved. Only a few recorded contests were held during this period: one was given in 216 B.C. between 22 pairs of gladiators; another, in 183 B.C., involved 60 pairs of gladiators. In 174 B.C. the tempo picked up when several gladiatorial contests were held that year, one lasting for three days and involving 74 gladiators. Others like this one may have been held, but no records survive.

Information pertaining to the development and expansion of gladiatorial contests from the middle of the second century to the beginning of the reign of Augustus (27 B.C.–14 A.D.) is meager. It is known that several large gladiatorial schools came into being and that many more schools, private as well as public, were added during the Empire. The slave Spartacus escaped from the gladiatorial school at Capua in 73 B.C. to lead a revolt that reached alarming proportions before it was finally quelled. More and more gladiators were involved as the games began to be extended over a longer period of time. In 65 B.C. Julius Caesar purchased so many gladiators that the Senate limited the number any private person could own.

Augustus provided funds for praetors to give gladiatorial games twice a year, with the stipulation that no more than 120 could be used each time. During the reign of Domitian (81–96 A.D.) the newly elected aediles were charged with the responsibility for the December games held throughout the Empire. Many other gladiatorial games—and they seemed always to be increasing—were provided by rich citizens, high officials, or emperors wanting to curry favor with the public. All were given on special occasions and were free to all. Private gladiatorial combats were held in addition to public ones, for many wealthy men maintained large numbers of gladiators. Gladiators also served as bodyguards for these same wealthy families.

Gladiators were drawn from the ranks of slaves, prisoners of war, criminals sentenced to death, or were occasional Roman citizens seeking adventure and excitement. One emperor, Commodus (180–192 A.D.), fought in the arena a few times. Gladiators were trained in schools, where they specialized in certain weapons and modes of fighting which determined their classification and opponents.

There were four principal types of gladiators: Retiarii, Samnites, Thracians, and Secutores. Those belonging to the Retiarius group fought with a net used to entangle their opponents; for a weapon they used a three-pronged harpoon (trident). The Samnites fought with a long sword and were protected by a large oblong shield, a visored helmet, a greave on the left arm, and the heavy sleeve on the right arm which all gladiators wore. They were heavily equipped. The Thracians wore greaves on both legs, a visor, carried a small shield, and fought with a curved sword. The Secutores, the chief opponents of the despised Retiarii, were armed with a sword, shield, visored helmet, and leg greaves.

Gladiatorial games began with a parade of the combatants in full armor and bearing their weapons. The participants marched around the arena led by a band playing appropriate music, perhaps stopping at one point to give the famous cry: *Ave, Imperator, morituri te salutant!* (Hail, Emperor, we who are about to die salute you!) Weapons were then examined and approved by the official in charge of the games. During the warm-up period prior to the start of the actual combat, mock fights of various kinds were held with blunt weapons, often to the accompaniment of music. With a somber musical flourish the first real contest was announced. Mood music may have been used throughout the contest to intensify the action (much as bands and flashing scoreboards are used in baseball parks today). Those who were wounded signaled to the crowd to be spared; often they were if they had put up a good fight. The dead or wounded were removed after each contest and new sand sprinkled on the blood-soaked sands of the arena before the next contest began. Especially keen interest was aroused when fighting occurred between different gladiator categories, such as a Thracian versus a Retarius.

The passion for all types of gladiatorial games was an ever-mounting element in the Empire period, so great that it easily overshadowed all forms of entertainment except chariot races and the more exotic and cruel forms of *venationes*. It is no wonder that the theatre, in order even to exist against this kind of competition, had to turn to huge spectacles involving casts of several hundreds, to coarse Atellan farces, to lewd mime shows, and to lascivious and pornographic pantomimes, as the entertainment tastes of jaded and satiated Romans degenerated. The decline of the literary Roman theatre as a vital art form almost parallels the development and expansion of gladiatorial contests and *venationes*.

VENATIONES

Another of the colorful and exciting spectacles introduced into Rome began when Marcus Fulvius Nobilior exhibited a number of wild animals in the Circus Maximus in 186 B.C. It was not long before larger exhibitions followed in which animals hunted other animals, or men hunted animals. Attempts were made to place beasts in their native habitats by adding shrubbery, trees, and hillocks—even decorating them—to provide the proper natural stage settings for the events. Soon there evolved a professional group of *bestiarii* drawn from condemned prisoners and prisoners of war who specialized in hunting and fighting with animals and were trained in special schools. On the social scale these men were a step or two below gladiators and several steps below the charioteers.

The earliest wild animals used in *venationes* came from the mountainous regions of northern Italy, Gaul, and Spain. In the fading years of the Republic and the early part of the Empire, as new territories in Africa and Asia were added, the more exotic and ferocious varieties of animals became available for the circuses and amphitheatres. Around the middle of the first century B.C. Pompey and Julius Caesar staged some of the most extravagant *venationes* ever given. Pompey's games utilized 600 lions, 20 elephants, and a mixture of 410 leopards and other animals all hunted by

Reconstruction of a *venatione*, featuring a variety of animals and hunters, as it may have been staged in the Colosseum. (From Romanus, *Antiquae Urbis Splendor* [1612].)

Amphitheatres at Capua (top) and Pozzuoli (bottom) showing central opening *(media via)*, which was used for moving scenery up from the region below the arena level, and openings in arena floor for accommodating animal cages, which came up from region below. (Photo Alinari.)

bestiarii armed with darts. At Caesar's games in 46 B.C. 400 lions were hunted as well as 40 elephants.

The full theatrical and spectacular potential of the *venationes* was not realized until the Flavian Amphitheatre opened in 80 A.D. Its vast underground labyrinth made possible the theatrical devices and machinery for staging and for making quick scene shifts that had been lacking in circuses. Probably a huge opening down the middle axis of the arena *(media via)*, such as is found in the amphitheatre at Capua and at Pozzuoli, was installed at the Flavian Amphitheatre for moving scenery up from beneath the arena to the floor level. This can be confirmed by a description of one of Nero's amphitheatrical spectacles where woods and fountains suddenly came into view as the earth seemed to open up. This setting was then supplied with suitable animals which emerged from trapdoors in the arena floor.

The utmost ingenuity was surely required by those who staged the 100-day festival given by Titus at the opening of the Flavian Amphitheatre. It was reported that in one day alone 5,000 wild animals were exhibited; in the course of the festival 9,000, including many varieties of tame and wild ones, were killed. The emperor Trajan topped this figure of slaughter in 109 A.D., when he celebrated the second Dacian victory with a four-month festival during which 11,000 animals were killed by various exotic means.

If ancient reports are correct, the amount and variety of entertainment available to Roman audiences in the Colosseum must have been immense. Aside from the gladiatorial contests and naumachiae, there were theatrical performances of a Grand Guignol character. Often, real torture was employed, instead of the illusionary kind, to illustrate mythological happenings, such as the magical gifts of Medea consuming Jason's new queen in a fiery inferno. There were bullfights; all types of animal-baiting and -hunting by *bestiarii* bedecked in most colorful garb amid forests and jungles made fantastically real. Animals were painted, decorated, and paraded; performing animals were trained to do unusual and prodigious feats; and tortures of all types were inflicted.

NAUMACHIAE

The gaudiest and most spectacular of all Roman paratheatricals were the naumachiae (ship battles). They were splendid reenactments of famous naval engagements for the entertainment of the Roman populace. Julius Caesar, or one of his staff members, was responsible for creating the first naumachia. It was given on an artificial lake which Caesar constructed on the Campus Martius in 46 B.C. In the same year he gave a series of games in order to win favor with the senators, many of whom felt he was determined to be a dictator and distrusted him. Caesar caused a Tyrian fleet to clash with an Egyptian fleet. Each was supplied with warships of

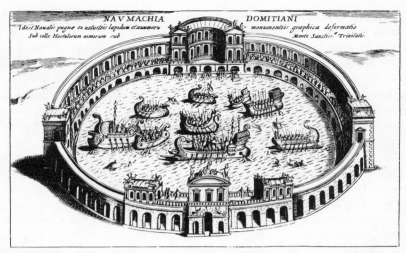

Reconstructions of naumachiae constructed by Domitian and Nero. (From Romanus, *Antiquae Urbis Splendor* [1612].)

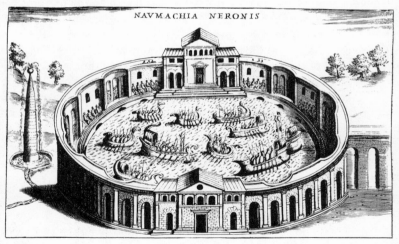

the bireme, trireme, and quadririme classes (two, three, and four banks of oars), manned by 2,000 oarsmen and 1,000 soldiers. A sizable battle was thus reenacted. In 43 B.C. this lake was drained as a health precaution, the result of an epidemic.

Augustus, in 2 B.C., gave in connection with the dedication of the Temple of Mars Ultor what was probably the second naumachia in ancient Rome, when he created a lake 1,800 feet long by 1,200 feet wide by digging out part of Caesar's gardens near the Tiber River and installing marble benches for spectators. On this occasion, in commemoration of the Battle of Salamis, the sea battle was between an Athenian and a Persian fleet consisting of 6,000 soldiers and 30 biremes and triremes, together with a number of smaller vessels.

To Claudius goes the credit for staging the greatest of all naumachiae. This one took place at one end of Lake Fucine, situated some 60 miles east of Rome, in 52 A.D. A total of 19,000 men (gladiators, condemned criminals, and prisoners of war rounded up from all parts of Italy) dressed as Rhodians and Sicilians boarded a fleet of 50 warships and joined combat in an area that gave plenty of room for maneuvering. The battle lasted from 10:00 a.m. until 3:00 p.m. That day, 3,000 men met their death, turning the lake red with blood.

The only naumachiae given in the Colosseum were held shortly after it opened. These are credited to the emperors Titus and Domitian. They must have been enormous undertakings and highly disruptive for other activities normally given there. Domitian must not have been too pleased with the results, for he soon had an artificial pond dug on the right bank of the Tiber River to house his naumachiae. There may have been one or two more basins for naumachiae constructed in Rome; however, the evidence about them is very sparse.

GAMES AND SPECTACLES IN RETROSPECT

The tremendous appeal and drawing power of Roman games and spectacles, with their competitive, brutal, and sadistic qualities, have been emphasized by historians. The paratheatrical qualities of personating, costuming, staging, and miming, as well as the pomp, ceremony, and ritual which surrounded these events, gave them a decided advantage over theatrical performances. Spectacles captured huge audiences. The competition was too much for the theatre to withstand. As a result, the theatre deteriorated rapidly when it started emulating some of the grosser aspects of the circuses and arenas.

NOTES

1. Among the Greek theatres converted by the Romans for gladiatorial contests and wild-beast combats were those at Assus, Magnesia, Pergamum, Corinth, and Tyndaris.
2. Ruins of more than 85 Roman amphitheatres have been discovered in

144 | GAMES AND SPECTACLES IN ROME

Europe, Africa, and Asia; 20 are located in North Africa alone.

3. Ludwig Friedländer, *Roman Life and Manners Under the Early Empire* (authorized trans. of 7th rev. and enlarged ed. by J. H. Freese and Leonard A. Magnus, *Sittengeschichte Romo,* II, 4–8; New York: Barnes & Noble, 1965). This is one of the finest and most complete accounts in English of Roman games and spectacles. See also J. P. V. D. Balsdon, *Life and Leisure in Ancient Rome* (London: Bodley Head, 1969), pp. 244–399; Jérôme Carcopino, *Daily Life in Ancient Rome: The People and the City at the Height of the Empire* (ed. with biblio. and notes by Henry T. Rowell and trans. from the French by E. O. Lorimer; New Haven: Yale University Press, 1960), pp. 202–247; Mary Johnston, *Roman Life* (Chicago: Scott, Foresman, 1957), pp. 269–303; and W. Warde Fowler, *Social Life at Rome in the Age of Cicero* (New York: Macmillan, 1913), pp. 285–318.

4. For a visual account, see the two filmstrips by James H. Butler, *Roman Circuses* and *Amphitheatres and Naumachiae* (Los Angeles: Olesen Films, 1959).

5. See Robert B. Montilla, "The Awnings of Roman Theatres and Amphitheatres," *Theatre Survey,* 10 (1969), 75–88.

Suggested Readings
and Filmstrips

THEATRE AND DRAMA

Allen, James Turney. *Stage Antiquities of the Greeks and Romans and their Influence.* New York: Longmans, Green, 1927. Reprinted by Cooper Square Publishers, New York, 1963.

Arnott, Peter D. *Greek Scenic Conventions in the Fifth Century B.C.* Oxford: Clarendon Press, 1962.

————*An Introduction to the Greek Theatre.* London and New York: Macmillan, 1959.

Beare, W. *The Roman Stage: A Short History of Latin Drama in the Time of the Republic.* 3rd ed.; New York: Barnes & Noble, 1963.

Bieber, Margarete. *The History of the Greek and Roman Theater.* 2nd ed. rev.; Princeton, N.J.: Princeton University Press, 1961.

Butler, James H. *The Ancient Greek Theatre of Epidauros; The Theatre of Dionysus, Part 1 and 2; The Roman Theatre of Orange; and The Greek Hellenistic Theatre of Priene.* 5 filmstrips; Los Angeles: Olesen Films, 1957.

————*Roman Circuses* and *Amphitheatres and Naumachiae.* 2 filmstrips; Los Angeles: Olesen Films, 1959.

Cornford, Francis M. *The Origin of Attic Comedy.* Ed. with foreword and additional notes by Theodor H. Gaster; New York: Anchor Books, 1961.

Duckworth, George E. *The Nature of Roman Comedy: A Study in Popular Entertainment.* Princeton, N.J.: Princeton University Press, 1952.

Else, Gerald F. *The Origin and Early Form of Greek Tragedy.* Cambridge, Mass.: Harvard University Press, 1965.

Flickinger, Roy C. *The Greek Theatre and Its Drama.* 6th ed. enlarged; Chicago: University of Chicago Press, 1960.

Haigh, A. E. *The Attic Theatre.* 3rd ed. rev. and in part rewritten by Sir Arthur W. Pickard-Cambridge; Oxford: Clarendon Press, 1907.

Hanson, John Arthur. *Roman Theater-Temples*. Princeton, N.J.: Princeton University Press, 1959.

Lawler, Lillian B. *The Dance of the Ancient Greek Theatre*. Iowa City: University of Iowa Press, 1964.

Pickard-Cambridge, Sir Arthur W. *Dithyramb, Tragedy and Comedy*. 2nd ed. by T. B. L. Webster; Oxford: Clarendon Press, 1962.

_____*The Dramatic Festivals of Athens*. Oxford: Clarendon Press, 1953; 2nd ed. by John Gould and D. M. Lewis, 1968.

_____*The Theatre of Dionysus in Athens*. Oxford: Clarendon Press, 1946.

Segal, Erich. *Roman Laughter: The Comedy of Plautus*. Cambridge, Mass.: Harvard University Press, 1968.

Sifakis, G. M. *Studies in the History of Hellenistic Drama*. London: University of London, Athlone Press, 1967.

Vitruvius, *Ten Books on Architecture*. Trans. by Morris Hickey Morgan; New York: Dover Publications, 1960.

Webster, T. B. L. *Greek Theatre Production*. London: Methuen, 1956; 2nd ed., 1970.

HISTORY AND GENERAL BACKGROUND

Andrews, Antony. *The Greeks*. London: Hutchinson, 1967.

Balsdon, J. P. V. D. *Life and Leisure in Ancient Rome*. London: Bodley Head, 1969.

Burn, A. R. *The Pelican History of Greece*. Baltimore: Penguin Books, 1966.

Carcopino, Jérôme. *Daily Life in Ancient Rome: The People and the City at the Height of the Empire*. Ed. with biblio. and notes by Henry T. Rowell and trans. from the French by E. O. Lorimer; New Haven: Yale University Press, 1960.

Finley, M. I. *The Ancient Greeks*. New York: Viking Press, 1963.

Friedländer, Ludwig. *Roman Life and Manners Under the Early Empire*. Authorized trans. of 7th rev. and enlarged ed. by J. H. Freese and Leonard A. Magnus, *Sittengeschichte Romo*, Vol. II; New York: Barnes & Noble, 1965.

Hatzfeld, Jean. *History of Ancient Greece*. Rev. by André Agemard, trans. by A. C. Harrison, ed. by E. H. Goddard; New York: Norton, 1966.

Johnston, Mary. *Roman Life*. Chicago: Scott, Foresman, 1957.

Roebuck, Carl. *The World of Ancient Times*. New York: Scribner's, 1966.

Tenney, Frank. *Life and Literature in the Roman Republic*. Berkeley: University of California Press, 1930.

Wycherley, R. E. *How the Greeks Built Cities*. 2nd ed.; London: Macmillan, 1962.

Chronology of Important Historical and Theatrical Events

GREECE

Dates preceded by an asterisk (*) indicate theatrical events.

4000–3000 B.C.	Neolithic Period.
3000–1200 B.C.	Minoan Period.
* ca. 2000 B.C.	"Theatral area" built at Phaestos, Crete.
1800–1500 B.C.	Most brilliant era of Cretan civilization.
* ca. 1600 B.C.	"Theatral area" built at Knossos, Crete.
1600–1400 B.C.	Linear A and B systems of writing.
ca. 1500 B.C.	Eruption of Island of Thera and destruction of everything on Crete.
1500–1100 B.C.	Mycenean civilization.
ca. 1250–1240 B.C.	Siege and destruction of Troy.
1200–800 B.C.	Dorian invaders settled at Corinth, Sicyon, Argos, etc.; Dark Age.
800–500 B.C.	Archaic Age.
776 B.C.	First Olympic games held.
750 B.C.	Origin of Greek alphabet; founding of Cumae.
750–500 B.C.	Age of Greek colonization: eastward to Black Sea, westward into Sicily and southern Italy; growth of Greek city-states.
734 B.C.	Founding of Syracuse.
700–550 B.C.	Homeric poems written.
650–500 B.C.	Age of tyrants.
650–600 B.C.	Invention of coinage.
* ca. 625–585 B.C.	Arion from Lesbos gave literary form to dithyrambs at Corinth.

147

594–593 B.C.   Solon's reforms.

* ca. 581 B.C.   Doric mimes came into being.

* ca. 581–560 B.C.   Susarion led choral performances.

* ca. 565–404 B.C.   Old Comedy.

546–527 B.C.   Perisistraids—tyrants.

* ca. 534 B.C.   City Dionysia established by Pisistratus; first tragic contest won by Thespis.

* ca. 530–ca. 440 B.C.   Epicharmus gave literary form to Doric mimes.

* 525/4–456 B.C.   Aeschylus.

* ca. 510 B.C.   Dithyrambic contests added to City Dionysia.

* 501 B.C.   Comedy officially made part of City Dionysia.

500–336 B.C.   Classical Period.

* 499/8 B.C.   Dramatic presentations moved to precinct of Dionysus on southwest slope of Acropolis.

499–494 B.C.   Ionian revolt.

* 497/6–406 B.C.   Sophocles.

* ca. 495 B.C.   Aeschylus added second actor.

490 B.C.   Battle of Marathon.

* 487/6 B.C.   Comedy officially recognized at City Dionysia.

* 485/4–406 B.C.   Euripides.

* 484 B.C.   Aeschylus won his first victory at City Dionysia.

480 B.C.   Battle of Thermopylae and Salamis.

477–461 B.C.   Delian League.

* 472 B.C.   Earliest extant Greek play, Aeschylus' *The Persians.*

* ca. 471–468 B.C.   Sophocles introduced third actor.

* 468 B.C.   Sophocles won his first victory.

463–431 B.C.   Public life of Pericles.

461–431 B.C.   Athenian Empire.

* 458 B.C.   Aeschylus' *The Oresteia.*

* 455 B.C.   First play of Euripides presented.

454/3 B.C.   Delian treasury moved to Athens.

* 449 B.C.   Contest of tragic actors instituted at City Dionysia.

447–431 B.C.   Construction of Parthenon.

* ca. 446 B.C.   Odeion built by Pericles.

* ca. 445 B.C.   Periclean reconstruction of Theatre of Dionysus; Lenaea moved to Theatre of Dionysus.

* ca. 445–ca. 388 B.C.   Aristophanes.

* ca. 442 B.C.   Contest of tragic playwrights and tragic actors began at Lenaea.

* ca. 441 B.C.   Sophocles' *Antigone.*

* 441 B.C.   Euripides won his first victory.

* ca. 432 B.C.   Contest of comic playwrights introduced at Lenaea.

* 431 B.C.   Euripides' *Medea.*

431–404 B.C.   Peloponnesian War.

* ca. 430 B.C.   *Mēchanē* may have come into use in Theatre of Dionysus.

429 B.C.   Death of Pericles.

428–421 B.C.	Cleon.
* 425 B.C.	Aristophanes' *The Acharnians.*
* 421–415 B.C.	Wooden stoa at Theatre of Dionysus replaced by stone stoa.
* 405 B.C.	Aristophanes' *The Frogs.*
404 B.C.	Athens fell to Sparta.
404–371 B.C.	Spartan Empire.
* 404–336 B.C.	Middle Comedy.
399 B.C.	Trial and death of Socrates.
* ca. 386 B.C.	Revival of classical Greek tragedies started at City Dionysia.
359–336 B.C.	Reign of Philip II of Macedon.
* ca. 342/1–ca. 293/4 B.C.	Menander.
338 B.C.	Battle of Chaeronea.
* ca. 338–326 B.C.	Lycurgean renovations of Theatre of Dionysus.
336–31 B.C.	Hellenistic Period; Hellenistic theatres came into being.
336–323 B.C.	Reign of Alexander the Great.
* 336–290 B.C.	New Comedy.
* 3rd cent. B.C.	Guilds of performing artists established.
* ca. 277 B.C.	Amphictyonic Decree gave privileged status to actors.
31 B.C.	Battle of Actium; end of Hellenistic Period.

ROME

Dates preceded by an asterisk (*) indicate theatrical or paratheatrical events. Dates preceded by a dagger (†) indicate emperors' reigns.

9th cent. B.C.	Etruscan colonization.
8th & 7th cent. B.C.	Greek colonization of eastern Sicily and southern Italy (gulf of Taranto and coast of Campania).
753 B.C.	Traditional date for founding of Rome.
750 B.C.	Greek founding of Cumae.
509 B.C.	Kings overthrown (last king, Tarquin); Republic formed.
509–264 B.C.	Early Roman Republic.
450 B.C.	Twelve Tables of Law.
390 B.C.	Sacking and burning of Rome by Gauls.
* 366 B.C.	Ludi Romani established as annual event.
* 364 B.C.	Theatrical performances added to Ludi Romani; Etruscan dancers invited to Rome to perform.
326–290 B.C.	The three Samnite Wars.
* 300 B.C.	Rhinton of Tarentum gave literary form to *phlyakes.*
* ca. 284–204 B.C.	Livius Andronicus, first Roman translator and adapter of Greek plays.
281–272 B.C.	War with King Pyrrhus and Tarentum.

* ca. 270–201 B.C. Gnaeus Naevius, Italy's first native dramatist.
* 264 B.C. First gladiatorial combat held in Rome.
264–241 B.C. First Punic War.
* ca. 254–ca. 184 B.C. Plautus (Titus Maccius Plautus), 20 of his comedies extant.

241 B.C. Western Sicily made first Roman province.
* 240 B.C. Livius Andronicus presented tragedy and comedy translated from Greek at Ludi Romani—first literary drama to reach Rome.

* 239–169 B.C. Quintus Ennius, dramatist.
238 B.C. Corsica and Sardinia became Roman provinces.
* 235 B.C. First play of Naevius produced at Rome.
* 221 B.C. Circus Flaminius built in Rome.
* ca. 220–130 B.C. Marcus Pacuvius, tragic dramatist.
* ca. 219–166 B.C. Statius Cascilius, comic dramatist.
218–202 B.C. Second Punic War.
* 206 B.C. Imprisonment of Naevius.
* ca. 205 B.C. Plautus' *The Braggart Warrior.*
202 B.C. Battle of Zama and defeat of Hannibal.
* 200–85 B.C. Golden Age of Roman drama.
200–168 B.C. Macedonian Wars.
200–150 B.C. Period of Senate supremacy and rapid colonization.

* ca. 185/4–159 B.C. Terence (Publius Terentius Afer), 6 of his comedies extant.

* 180 B.C. Marcus Fulvius Nobilior presented first exhibition of animals *(venationes)* in Rome.

* 170–ca. 86 B.C. Lucius Accius, dramatist.
* 150–? B.C. Lucius Afranius, writer of *fabulae togatae.*
149–146 B.C. Third Punic War.
148 B.C. Macedonia annexed.
146 B.C. Corinth and Carthage destroyed; Africa annexed as Roman province; fall of Numantia, Spain; tribunate of Tiberius Gracchus, his land reforms and murder.

* ca. 130–ca. 62 B.C. Roscius (Quintus Roscius Gallus), most famous actor.

121 B.C. Organization of Roman province of Provence (France).

111–105 B.C. War with Jugurtha, King of Numidia, Africa.
* 106–43 B.C. Decimus Laberius gave literary form to mimes.
* ca. 90 B.C. Mime writers Pomponius and Novius.
90–88 B.C. Revolt of Italian allies and grant of citizenship to all in Italy south of Po River.

87–84 B.C. First Mithridatic War—beginning of decline of Greece until early Empire days.

82–79 B.C. Dictatorship of Sulla, powers of Senate restored.
77–71 B.C. War against Sertorius in Spain, Pompey in command.

* ca. 75 B.C.	First Roman odeum built at Pompeii.
* 73–71 B.C.	Revolt of Spartacus, his escape from gladiatorial school at Capua and defeat by Crassus.
70 B.C.	Consulship of Pompey and Crassus; trials of Verras and rise of Cicero as public figure.
* ca. 70 B.C.	Amphitheatre at Pompeii, first and oldest surviving Roman amphitheatre.
63 B.C.	Catiline's conspiracy; Cicero's consulship.
60 B.C.	First triumvirate: Pompey, Crassus, and Caesar.
59 B.C.	Consulship of Caesar.
58–50 B.C.	Caesar's conquest of Gaul.
* 55 B.C.	Theatre of Pompey, Rome's first permanent stone theatre, opened.
49–45 B.C.	Civil War.
47–44 B.C.	Dictatorship of Caesar.
* 46 B.C.	Caesar staged first naumachia in Rome.
45 B.C.	Introduction of Julian calendar.
44 B.C. (March 15)	Assassination of Caesar.
43 B.C.	Second triumvirate: Antony, Octavian, and Lepidus.
42 B.C.	Battle of Philippi.
31 B.C.	Battle of Actium.
30 B.C.	Death of Antony and Cleopatra.
† 27 B.C.–14 A.D.	Principate of Augustus.
* 22 B.C.	Pylades and Bathyllus introduced pantomime into Rome.
* ca. 16–ca. 13 B.C.	Vitruvius, *On Architecture*—section of book devoted to Greek and Roman theatres.
* 13 B.C.	Theatre of Balbus opened in Rome.
* 11 B.C.	Theatre of Marcellus, last theatre to be built in Rome.
* ca. 4 B.C.–65 A.D.	Seneca (Lucius Annaeus Seneca), philosopher and playwright, 9 of his tragedies extant.
* 2 B.C.	Augustus staged second naumachia.
† 14–37 A.D.	Principate of Tiberius.
†37–41 A.D.	Gaius (Caligula).
† 41–54 A.D.	Claudius.
* 52 A.D.	Claudius staged greatest naumachia of ancient times on Lake Fucine.
† 54–68 A.D.	Nero.
64 A.D.	Great fire of Rome.
† 69–79 A.D.	Vespasian.
† 79–81 A.D.	Titus.
79 A.D.	Eruption of Mt. Vesuvius destroyed Pompeii and Herculaneum.
* 80 A.D.	Flavian Amphitheatre completed in Rome, later called the Colosseum.
† 81–96 A.D.	Domitian.
† 96–98 A.D.	Nerva.

† 98–117 A.D.   Trajan.
† 117–138 A.D.   Hadrian.
† 138–161 A.D.   Antoninus Pius.
† 161–180 A.D.   Marcus Aurelius.
  161–180 A.D.   Parthian and Danubian Wars.
  166 A.D.   Plague.
† 180–192 A.D.   Commodus.
† 192–211 A.D.   Septimius Severus.
* 200 A.D.   Women gladiators prohibited.
† 211–217 A.D.   Caracalla.
  212 A.D.   Citizenship granted to all free inhabitants of Empire.
* ca. 235 A.D.   Theatre of Marcellus abandoned.
  270–275 A.D.   Aurelian restores Empire.
† 285–305 A.D.   Diocletian (Maximian, Galerius, Constantius)—tetrarchy.
† 307–324 A.D.   Constantine the Great and Licinius.
*309 A.D.   Circus Maxentius built just outside Rome.
  313 A.D.   Edict of Milan (freedom of worship).
† 324–337 A.D.   Constantine sole emperor.
  330 A.D.   Founding of Constantinople.
† 337–360 A.D.   Constantius.
  378 A.D.   Battle of Andrianople.
  380–430 A.D.   St. Jerome, St. Ambrose, and St. Augustine.
  395 A.D.   Roman Empire divided into Eastern and Western Empires.

Western Empire

† 395–423 A.D.   Honorius.
* 399 A.D.   Last gladiatorial school abolished.
* 404 A.D.   Edict by Honorius stopped gladiator games in Western Roman Empire.
  410 A.D.   Alaric and Goths capture Rome.
  429 A.D.   Vandal invasion of Africa.
  453 A.D.   Death of Attila the Hun.
* 549 A.D.   Last chariot race held in Rome.

Eastern Empire

† 395–408 A.D.   Arcadius.
† 408–450 A.D.   Theodosius II.
† 527–565 A.D.   Justinian, last Roman emperor.
  527–1453 A.D.   *Byzantine Empire.*

Index

Abydos Passion Play, 1
Accius, Lucius, 81, 82
Acharnians, The (Aristophanes), 17, 20, 52, 57, 65, 68
Acrobatics, 18, 76, 119, 128
Acropolis, 19, 29, 33, 51, 52, 54
Acting, 12, 17, 18, 31, 37, 40, 56, 57, 58-59, 60, 65-66, 78, 112-115, 119-123
   styles, 65-66, 114-115, 119-122
Actius, 114
Actor-managers, 111-114
Actors:
   Atellan farce, 88, 112-113, 118-123
   Greek comedy, 22-24, 27, 29-30, 33, 40-41, 52-54, 56-57, 60-62, 64, 65, 68
   Greek mime, 17-19
   Greek tragedy, 6-8, 9-12, 27, 29-30, 33, 40-41, 43, 52-57, 60, 62-63, 64, 68
   phlyake, 77-78
   Roman, 111, 112-113, 115, 125, 126
   Roman mime, 75-76, 114, 119-120
   Roman pantomine, 76-77, 119-122
   satyr drama, 14, 30, 33, 40-41, 53-54, 56, 60, 62
Adelophoe (Terence), 85
Adonis, 12
Adrastus, 3
Aediles, 111, 137
Aegean islands, 27, 70, 103
Aegis, 65
Aeidein, 6, 16

Aencodae (Accius), 82
Aeropagus, 52
Aeschylean drama, 11, 55, 59
Aeschylus, 6-9, 14, 18, 29, 33, 48, 55-57, 60, 67
Aesopus, 112-114, 120, 126
Afranius, Lucius, 83
Africa (North Africa), 27, 70, 93, 103-104, 127, 139
Agamemnon (Aeschylus), 8
Agamemnon (Seneca), 82
Agatharchus, 67
Agave, 120
Agōn, 18, 22
Agonothētēs, 55, 56
Agora, 29, 45, 52
Ajax (Sophocles), 9, 68
Alcestis (Euripides), 10
Alcestis (Phrynichus), 7
Alcmaeon at Corinth (Euripides), 10, 68
Alexander the Great, 23, 41, 58, 121
Alexis of Thurii, 24
Alta, 83
Altar, 41, 43, 52, 53, 67, 91, 123
   See also *Thymele*
Ameipsias, 19
Amphi-, 133
Amphiaros, Sanctuary of, 45
Amphitheatres, 103, 127, 133-136, 140-141
Amphitryon (Plautus), 84
Analemma, 37, 43
Andria (Terence), 85
Andromache (Euripides), 10, 68

153

Andromeda (Euripides), 64
Andronicus, Livius, 78-80, 88, 90
Animal baiting and hunting, 94, 99, 100, 109-110, 126, 127-128, 134, 135, 139-141
   See also Venationes
Animals, performing, 119
Antigone (Sophocles), 9, 12
Antiphanes, 24
Antipho, 112
Apelles, 114
Apennines, 72
Apollo, 16, 65, 91
Appian Way, 128
Appolinares, Ludi, 110
Arbitration, The (Menander), 25
Archimimus, 119
Archon (*basileus eponynus*), 9, 54, 55, 56, 57, 70
Arena, 118, 129-130, 132, 133-136, 138, 139, 141, 143
Ares, 89
Argos, 14
   odeum, 93
   theatre, 30, 44, 46, 93
Arion of Lesbos, 3, 5
Aristophanes, 17, 19, 20, 22-23, 29, 48, 52, 57, 92
Aristotle, 5, 9, 16
Arles:
   amphitheatre, 98, 128, 133
   theatre, 103, 124
Arno River, 72
Artists of Dionysus (guild), 51, 58
Asclepius, 36
Asia, 127, 139
Asia Minor, 4, 44
   See also Ionia
Aspendos, theatre, 104
Assus, theatre, 44
Atella, 74
Atellan farces, 73-75, 77, 83-84, 88, 94, 97, 112, 114, 117, 118-119, 121-123, 126, 138
Athena, 3, 10, 41, 65
Athenodorus, 59
Athens (Athenian), 3, 5, 7-9, 11-12, 16

17, 19-24, 29, 36, 44-45, 50-52, 53, 54, 55-56, 58, 69-70, 87, 93, 143
   odeum, 93
   theatre, 29, 44, 51
Atilius, 112
Atreus, 114
Attic districts, 50
Attic tribes, 53, 54, 66
Attica, 16, 51
Audience, 7, 15, 18, 22-25, 29-30, 40, 52-55, 62-65, 68-70, 77, 83, 85, 88, 91, 93, 96, 105, 112-114, 119, 120, 123, 125-126, 128, 140, 143
   See also Spectators
Auditorium, 96
Augustus, 77, 93, 94, 103-104, 110-111, 130, 137, 142
Aulaeum, 107, 124
Aulularia (Plautus), 84, 91
Aurelius, Marcus, 128
Aventine Hills, 128
Awnings, 105, 136

Bacchae, The (Euripides), 10, 13-14
Bacchantes (maenads), 4, 51, 79
Bacchus, 79, 120-121
Balbus, theatre, 96, 97, 101
Banqueters, The (Aristophanes), 57
Bathyllus, 77, 121
Bdelycleon, 21, 22
Beasts, The (Crates), 19
Bema, 99
Benches, 36, 41, 70
Benevento, theatre, 103
Bestiarii, 134, 139, 141
Bibliotheca Bodmeriana of Cologny, 25
Birds, 17, 18, 65
Birds, The (Aristophanes), 17, 20, 57
Bireme, 142-143
Bononia, 75
Boulē, 54
Bouleuterion at Miletus, 93
Boxers, 85, 110
Braggart Warrior, The (Plautus), 84, 92
Bride of Pappus, The, 75
Brigadiers, The (Eupolis), 19
Brindisi, 82

Broadway theatres, 90
Bronteion, 68
Brothel, The, 75
Brothers, The (Terence), 85
Brutus (Accius), 82
Bucco, 75, 119
Bucco the Gladiator, 75

Cadmus, 120
Caduceus, 65
Caesar, Julius, 134, 137, 139, 141, 143
Caesilius Statius, 83, 120, 122
Calabria, 79
Caligula, 114, 122, 128
Campania, 73, 74, 133
Campus Martius, 94-95, 96, 141
Cantica, 80, 85, 115
Capitol, 130
Captives, The (Plautus), 84
Capua, 74, 133, 137, 139
  amphitheatre, 134, 141
Carceres, 129, 130
Carthage (Carthaginians), 79, 80, 84, 125
Carthaginian, The (Plautus), 84
Casina (Plautus), 84
Casket, The (Plautus), 84
Cassandra, 68
Cato, 81, 82, 125
Cavea, 92, 96-98, 101, 104-105
Centunculus, 12, 123
Cereales, Ludi, 110
Chaera, 113
Chaeronea, theatre, 30
Chariot races, 109, 128-132
Charioteers, 128-132, 138, 139
Charon's steps, 68, 99, 123
Cheiron, 89
Cheironomia, 59, 60
Chionides, 16, 19
Chiton, 62-63, 64, 65, 117
Chlamys, 63, 117
Choerilus, 7, 29, 56
Choral ode, 7, 22, 60
Choregoi, 53, 54, 55-56, 66-67
Choreutai, 59

Chorodidaskaloi, 59
Chorus, 3-8, 10, 11, 12, 16, 18, 19-24, 30-31, 40, 46, 48, 52-53, 54, 56-57, 59-62, 65-67, 69, 77
  leader, 56, 60
  teacher, 59
Cicero, 82, 113-115, 124, 126
Cinius, 112
Cinyras, 12
Circus, 91, 94, 105-106, 127-132, 133, 139, 143
Citharae, 120
City Dionysia: *See* Dionysia, City
Claques, 125
Classical theatres, characteristics, 29-31
Clastidium (Naevius), 80
Claudius, 122, 143
Cleander, 56
Cleidemides, 57
Cleisthenes of Sicyon, 3
Cleon, 20, 22, 52
Clouds, The (Aristophanes), 19, 20, 62, 68
Clytemnestra, 8, 68
Coliseum (Los Angeles), 133
Coloneus, 9
Colonnade, 48, 96, 98, 99, 103, 106
Colosseum (Rome), 79, 94, 130-136, 139-140, 143
  See also Flavian Amphitheatre
Columns, 39, 42, 43, 67, 88, 104, 123, 130, 136
Comedy, Greek:
  Middle, 23-24, 57
  New, 24-25, 40, 46, 62, 80
  Old, 3, 5, 16-22, 33, 48, 51-52, 53, 54, 55-59, 62-66, 69
Comedy, Roman, 73-85, 92, 110, 111-117
Comedy of Asses, The (Plautus), 84
Commèdia dell'Arte, 76
Commodus, 137
Connos, The (Ameipsias), 19
Constantine, 130
Consuls, 111, 130
Consus, 110
Contamination, 85
Corbels, 105, 136

Corinth, 2, 3, 5
  odeum, 93
  theatre, 44-46, 93
Corinthian columns, 96, 136
Corinthian vase, 17
Coronation Festival Play, 1
Costumes, 6, 57, 61-65, 67, 78, 115-117,
  120, 122-123, 127
Cothurni, kothornoi, 63, 117-118
Craig, Edward Gordon, 56
Crates, 19
Cratinus, 19
Creon, 9
Cretan theatral areas, 28-29
Cumae, 72
Curculio (Plautus), 84
Curio, Gaius Scribonius, 88
Curtains, 92, 124
Curule, 111
Cyclops, The (Euripides), 10, 15
Cymbals, 120
Cytheris, 120

Dacian victory, 141
Danaids, The (Phrynichus), 7
Dance, 1-7, 12, 17, 18, 20, 22, 28, 30, 48,
  51, 53-54, 56, 59-60, 65, 73, 74, 76-
  77, 79, 85, 87, 115, 119-120
De Architectura (Vitruvius), 101, 102
Decius (Accius), 82
Deikelistai, 18
Delos, 55
  theatre, 44, 45, 46
Delphi, theatre, 44, 48
Demarchus, 55
Deme, 5, 9, 55
Demes, The (Eupolis), 19
Demetrius (poet), 14
Demetrius (Roman actor), 114
Demosthenes, 59, 70
Deus ex machina, 10, 68
Deuteragōnistēs, 57, 58
Diazoma, 34, 36-37, 41, 44
Didaskaloi, 57, 65, 67
Dionysalexandros (Cratinus), 19
Dionysia (mime player), 120

Dionysia:
  City, 3-4, 6, 8-9, 15-18, 50-56, 66,
    69-70, 92
  Rural, 50-51, 55
  See also Lenaea
Dionysian ceremonies, 29
Dionysian cult, 4, 16, 52, 61, 79
Dionysian festivals, 3, 50-55
Dionysian mysteries, 51
Dionyso, 5
Dionysus:
  god, 3, 4, 6, 7, 52, 53, 60, 66
  temple, 33, 44, 52
  theatre, 29, 31-36, 44, 45, 49, 52, 67-
    68, 69, 70, 92, 97, 99, 127
Dionysus Eleuthereus, 29, 33, 52-53
"Dionysus, The Artists of," 51, 58
Diphilus (actor), 112
Diphilus (playwright), 25
Dithyrambos, 3
Dithyrambs, 4-6, 13-14, 33, 50, 53-54, 66,
  69
  contests, 51-52
  in production, 66-67
Diuerbia, 115
Doctors, foolish, 18
Dodona, theatre, 44, 48
Dominus gregis, 111
Domitian, 120, 137, 142-143
Doors, doorways, 31, 39, 40, 42-43, 46,
  48, 88, 90, 91, 92, 94, 97, 100, 103,
  104, 105, 115, 123
Dorian Greeks, 72
Dorian "mode," 60
Doric columns, 96, 136
Doric mimes, farces, 3, 16-18, 67, 75-76,
  79
Dossenus (Manducus), 74, 75, 119
Dressing rooms, 33, 142
Dromos, 128
Drunkards, 18, 21
Dugga, theatre, 104, 124
Dyskolos, The (Menander), 25

Ecclesiasterion at Priene, 93
Ecclesiazusae, The (Aristophanes), 20, 24
Egypt, 15, 45

Egyptian fleet, 142
Egyptian plays, 1
Ekklēsia, 53
Ekkyklema, 68
Electra (Euripides), 10, 59, 68
Electra (Sophocles), 9, 59, 68
Eleusinian mysteries, 6, 55, 61
Eleusis, 8, 51
   theatre, 51
Eleutherae, 53
Elis, theatre, 68
Embolima, 59
Empire, Roman, 72, 75, 77, 82, 101, 104,
     107, 110, 112, 114, 117, 119, 120,
     126, 127, 128, 130, 132, 137, 138
Ennius, Quintus, 82
Ephesus, 41, 92
   odeum, 93
   theatre, 44, 46, 93, 101
Epic, 5, 6, 12
Epicharmus, 17-18
Epidauros:
   festival, 47
   odeum, 93
   theatre, 44, 46, 93, 101
   93
Epidicus (Plautus), 84
Epigenes, 3
Episodes, 12, 40
Equestrian rank, 135
Eretria, theatre, 44, 46, 68
Eros (Roman actor), 112
Ethōs, 60
Etruria, 73, 133
Etruscan dances, 72-73, 87, 91, 133
Etruscans, 73, 128
Eumenides, The (Aeschylus), 8
Eunuch, The (Terence), 85, 111
Eupolis, 19, 20, 28
Euripides, 7, 9-12, 15, 20, 22-23, 29, 40,
     47-48, 57, 64, 68, 82, 85
Europe, 127
Exposition, 12

Fabula Atellana: See Atellan farces
Fabula palliata, 83, 118
Fabula praetexta, 80-85, 118

Fabula togata, 83, 118
Fall of Miletus, The (Phrynichus), 7
Farces: *See* Atellan farces; Doric mimes
Fascinum, 73
Favor (mime player), 120
Fertility rites, 4, 16
Fescennine verses, 72-73
Fescennium, 73
Festivals, 6, 47, 109-111
   See also Dionysia; Lenaea
Fiesole, theatre, 103, 104
Finances for *ludi,* 111
Fire-eating, 119
Flaminius, Circus, 91, 94, 128
Flatterers, The (Eupolis), 19
Flavian Amphitheatre, 133-134, 139-140
   See also Colosseum
Flora, temple, 91
Florales, Ludi, 76, 110
Flutes, flute players, 13, 14, 16, 22, 50,
     53, 56, 58, 60, 66, 69, 73, 76, 120,
     130
Foot clapper, 120, 122
Foot-races, 128
Forum, 91, 103, 114, 133
France, 103, 133
Frogs, The (Aristophanes), 20, 57
Fucine, Lake, 143
Funebres, Ludi (funeral games), 85, 110,
     133

Gallery, 96
Games and spectacles, 110, 127-144
Gateways, 31, 129
Gaul, 103, 139
Gestures, 6, 59-60, 65, 73, 76-77, 78, 112,
     120
   symbolic, 59, 60
Girl from Samos, The (Menander), 25
Gladiator, 104, 127, 133, 137-138, 143
Gladiatorial games, contests, 85, 89, 99,
     100, 109, 126, 133-134, 137-138, 143
Gladiatorial schools, 104, 137
Glutton, 18
Glyco, 114
Gorgon's head, 65
Greater Dionysia: *See* Dionysia, City

Greaves, 138
Greco-Roman theatres, 80, 97-101, 103, 104, 107
Greek National Theatre, 47-48
Greek theatre festivals, 48-55
Greek theatres, ancient, 27-48

Hannibal, 80, 84, 124
Harlequin, 123
Haunted House, The (Plautus), 84
Heauton Timorumenos (Terence), 85
Hecuba (Euripides), 10
Hecyra (Terence), 85
Helen (Euripides), 10
Hellenistic garden-park, 96
Hellenistic theatres, 31, 34, 39-48, 67-68, 88, 90, 91, 94, 98-99, 100, 107
Hellespont Guild, 58
Hephaestus, 89
Hera, 89
Heracleidae, The (Euripides), 10, 47
Heracles (Euripides), 10
Herald, 8
Hercules (Herakles), 65, 118
Hercules Furens, 121
Hercules on Oeta (Seneca), 82
Hermes, 16, 65
Hermione, Claudia, 119
Herodas, 17
Herodes Atticus, odeum and theatre, 48, 93
Hesione, 14
Hilarotragodia, 77
Himation, 63, 64, 117
Hippodrome, 127, 128
Hippolytus (Euripides), 10, 68
Hippos, 128
Histrio, 73, 112
Homer, 5, 7, 80
Homeric Hymn to Hermes, The, 15-16
Horace, 124
Horse races, 128
Hylas, 122
Hymns, 2
Hypokritēs, 56

Icaria, 5, 16, 17

theatre, 51
Ichneutai, The (Sophocles), 9, 15
Ikria, 29
Iliad, The (Homer), 6, 12
Impersonation, 4, 5-6
Improvisation, 3, 5, 18, 19, 76
Ion (Euripides), 10
Ionia, 27, 41, 58
Ionia Guild, 58
Ionic columns, 96, 136
Ionic "mode," 60
Iphigenia in Aulis (Euripides), 10
Iphigenia in Tauris (Euripides), 10
Ismene, 12
Ister, 73
Isthmian Guild, 58
Italian mimes, 76
Italian Renaissance, 27, 103
Italy, 27, 70, 72, 75, 76, 77, 79, 93, 103, 107, 133, 139, 143

Jason, 11, 141
Juggling, 18, 76, 119
Jupiter, 110
Justinian, 120
Juvenal, 114, 128

Kalpis vase, 13
Keraunoskopeion, 68
Knights, The (Aristophanes), 20
Knossos, 28
Kōmoi, 16, 51
Kōmōidia, 16
Kōmos, 16, 18, 22, 51
Konistra, 100
Kordax, 60
Koryphaios, 56, 60
Kothornoi, cothurni, 63, 117-118

Laberius, Decimus, 76, 120
Labes, 22
Lake Fucine, 143
Latimus, 120
Latin, 74, 79, 83, 115
Leda and the Swan, 77
Lenaea, 9, 19, 50-56
Lenaean theatre, 52

Lenai, 51
Leonidaion hostel, 45
Leptis Magna, theatre, 104
Libation Bearers, The (Aeschylus), 8, 68
Libretto, 120
Lightning mechanism, 68, 124
Livy, 72-73, 91
Logeion, 42-43
Ludi, 76, 79-80, 85, 91, 109-111
Ludi circenses, 127
Ludi scaenici, 91, 98, 109-111, 127
"Lycurgean Theatre," 34-35, 67
   See also Dionysus, theatre
Lydian "mode," 60
Lyon, theatre, 103
Lyre, 16, 120
Lyric poetry, 5
Lysistrata (Aristophanes), 20, 57, 59

Maccius: *See* Plautus
Maccus, 75, 83, 119
Maccus the Soldier, 75
Macedon (Macedonians), 23, 24, 80, 124
Mad Hercules, The (Seneca), 82
Maenads (bacchantes), 4, 51, 79
Magalenses, Ludi, 85, 110
Magic, 119
Magistrates, 111, 135
Magna Graecia, 74, 75, 77
Magnes, 16, 19
Magnesia, theatre, 44, 68, 99, 100, 101
Man Who Didn't Like People, The (Menander), 25
Managers and actors, 112-114
Manducus (Dossenus), 74, 75, 119
Map, 2
Marathon, 3
   Battle of, 5, 8
Marcellus, 94
   theatre, 96-97, 98, 100, 101
Masks,' 3, 6, 15, 17, 18, 21, 57, 60, 61, 62, 63, 66, 67, 75, 76, 77, 78, 115-117, 118, 119, 120, 121, 123
Maxentius, Circus, 128, 130
Maximus, Circus, 91, 128-130, 139
Mēchanē, 10-11, 67-68
Medea, 10-11, 141

Medea (Euripides), 10
Medea (Seneca), 82
Media via, 139
Megalopolis, 93
   theatre, 44, 46
Megara, 17, 18
Megarian mimes, 16, 17
Menaechmi (Plautus), 84
Menander, 25, 40-41, 63, 85
Menester, 122
Merchant, The (Plautus), 84
Messalina, 122
Messenger, 8, 12
Metae, 129
Metelli, 80
Methyse, 4
Middle Ages, 85
Miles Gloriosus (Plautus), 84, 92
Miletus, 44, 46, 93, 101
   odeum, 93
   theatre, 44, 46, 101
Mime, 16, 17, 18, 75, 76, 94, 107, 110, 117-122, 123, 125-126, 138, 143
Mimeisthai, 17, 75
Mimos, 17
Mimus, 75
Mind-reading, 119
Minoan civilization, 28
Minturno, theatre, 103
Minucius, 112
Missus, 129
Mother-in-Law, The (Terence), 85
Mt. Chynortion, 36
Mount Etna, 15
Mumming (revels), 3, 16, 18
Munera, 127
Music, 5, 12, 50, 60, 65, 66, 73, 74, 80, 85, 93, 115, 138
Mussolini, 98
Mykale marble, 41
Myrino, 62
Myth, mythology, 12, 15, 18, 19, 77, 120, 121

Naevius, Gnaeus, 80, 111
Naples, 74, 134
Naumachiae, 127, 134, 140-143

Neighbors, The (Crates), 19
Nemean Guild, 58
Neoptolemus, 59
Nero, 78, 98, 99, 114, 132, 133, 134, 139, 142
Neronis, Circus, 128, 130-131
Nerva, 128
New Pleuron, theatre, 44, 46
Nicostratus, 57
Nimes, amphitheatre, 133
Nobilior, Marcus Fulvius, 139
Non-Combatants, The (Eupolis), 20
Nouveau riche, 125
Novius, 75

Ode, 7
Odeion, odeum, 33, 53, 93-94
Odysseus, 15
Odyssey, The (Homer), 6, 15
Oedipus (Seneca), 82
Oedipus at Coloneus (Sophocles), 9
Oedipus the King (Sophocles), 9, 12, 55
Oeniadae, theatre, 44, 46
Ōidē, 93
Olympia, 45
On the Chorus (Sophocles), 10
Onkos, 40, 62, 117-118
Onomasticon (Pollux), 61
Oracles, 9
Orange, theatre, 104-107, 124
Orators, 114
Orcheisthai, 6
Orchestra, 6, 29, 30, 31, 33, 34, 36, 37, 41, 42, 44, 45, 46, 48, 49, 53-57, 60, 61, 68, 70, 92, 93, 94, 96, 98, 99, 100, 101, 103, 105, 106
Oresteia, The (Aeschylus), 8, 33, 57
Orestes (Euripides), 8, 10, 11, 59
Oropus, theatre, 39, 43, 44, 45, 46, 100
Ostia, theatre, 103, 104, 118
Ovid, 82, 121, 124

Pacuvius, Marcus, 81, 82
Palatine Hills, 128
Palla, pallium, 118
Pamphilus, 112
Panathenaea, festival, 3, 6

Panegyrics, 121
Panem et circences, 128
Pan's pipes, 120
Pantomime, 72, 76-77, 94, 107, 110, 117-118, 120-122, 123, 126, 138
Pantomimus, 76-77, 114, 120-121, 125
Panurgus, 112
Pappus, 75, 119
Papyrus, 15
Parabasis, 18, 22, 23, 69
Parasites, 18, 23, 114
Paraskenia, 31, 34, 67, 97, 105
Paratheatrical entertainment: *See* Games and spectacles
Paris (pantomimist), 79, 122
Parodos (entrance song), 12, 18, 22, 60
Parodos (lateral entrances into the theatre), 30-31, 37, 43, 97
Passageways, 34, 41, 68, 96, 128, 133
Patras, odeum and theatre, 93
Paulus, Aemelius, 85
Peace (Aristophanes), 19, 20
Peace of Nicias, 19
Peliades (Euripides), 10
Pellio, T. Publilius, 111-112
Peloponnesian War, 19, 20, 52, 53, 56, 70
Peloponnesus, 14, 15, 18, 36, 46
Pentheus, 79, 120
Pera, Decimus, 133
Pera, Marcus, 133
Pergamum:
    odeum, 93
    theatre, 44, 46, 68, 93
Perge, theatre, 44
Periaktoi, 39, 40, 68, 103, 123
Periander of Corinth, 2
"Periclean Theatre," 34
Pericles, 19, 33, 67
    odeum, 33, 53, 93
Periplecomenus, 92
Persia (Persians), 3, 8, 143
Persian Wars, 7, 8
Persians, The (Aeschylus), 8, 12, 57, 84
Phaedra, 11
Phaedra (Seneca), 82
Phaedrus, 99, 124

Phaestos, 28
Phallic rites, 16, 18, 51
Phallic songs, 3, 5
Phallus, 16, 17, 64, 65, 67, 123
Phereae, 12
Philemon, 25
Philhellenism movement, 124
Philocleon, 21-22
Philocles, 55
Philoctetes (Sophocles), 9
Phlius, 14
Phlyakes, 74, 77-78, 79
    stages, 88-90, 92, 107
    vase paintings, 78, 89
Phoenician Women, The (Euripides), 10
Phoenician Women, The (Phrynichus), 7
Phoenician Women, The (Seneca), 82
Phormio (Terence), 85
Phrygian "mode," 60
Phrynichus, 7, 56
Pimp, The, 101
Pinakes, 39, 40, 42, 43, 48, 67
Piraeus:
    Dionysian festival, 51
    theatre, 44
Pisistratus, 3, 6, 52
Pius, Antonius, 128
Plautine-Terentine theatre, 91-92, 93
Plautus, 40, 76, 83-84, 90, 91, 92, 112, 115
Plebeians, 135
Plebeii, Ludi (plebeian games), 92, 110
Plutarch, 9, 93, 114
Plutus (Aristophanes), 20, 24
Pnyx, 52
Podium, 100, 129, 135
Polis, 55
Pollux, Julius, 61, 67, 68, 117
Polus, 59
Polyclitus the Younger, 36
Polyphemus (cyclops), 15
Pompa circensis, 130
Pompeian Porticus, 96
Pompeii, 98
    amphitheatre, 133-134
    odeum, 88, 90, 93, 97, 107
    theatre, 44, 90, 95, 97, 104, 124, 125

Pompey, 94, 139
    theatre, 90, 93, 94-96, 101, 104, 124
Pomponius, 75
Populus, 128
Porticus, 96, 97, 98, 104, 106
Pot of Gold, The (Plautus), 84, 91
Pozzuoli, amphitheatre, 134, 139, 141
Praecinctio, 94, 96, 97, 135
Praenestine Cista, 113
Praetors, 111, 130, 137
Pratinas, 7, 14, 29, 56
Priene, 41, 93
    theatre, 31, 41-44, 45, 46, 101
Proagōn, 53, 92
Prodicus, 11
Producers, 111-112
Proedria, 41
Prologues, 5, 10, 12, 85, 91
Prometheus Bound (Aeschylus), 8, 57
Pronomos, 14, 15
Props, stage, 46, 54, 67, 92, 119, 123
Proskenion, 31, 36, 67
Proskenion-logeion, 39, 42, 45
Prōtagōnistēs, 57, 58
Protagoras, 11
Pseudolus (Plautus), 84
Pulcher, Claudius, 87
Pulpitum, 96, 98, 101
Punic Wars, 79, 80, 124
Pylades, 77, 121, 122
Pyrgopolynices, 92
Pyrrhic dances, 79
Pyrrhic War, 75

Quadririme, 142
Quintilian, 112, 114

Ramps, 37, 46, 90, 91, 100, 123
Recitations, tragic, 78, 126
Renaissance, 83, 85, 103
Republic, Roman, 72, 75, 128, 133, 139
Retiarii, 138
Revels, revellers, 4, 16
Rhamnus, 51
Rhapsōidia, rhapsodists, 3, 6, 10, 50, 58
Rhesus (Euripides), 11
Rhinthon of Tarentum, 77

Rhodians, 143
Rites, 6
Romani, Ludi, 79-80, 85, 110
Rome, 25, 56, 72, 73, 74, 77, 78, 79, 80, 81, 83, 84, 85, 87, 92, 94, 95, 103, 109, 117, 124, 126, 127, 128, 132, 133, 134, 137, 143
Romulus (Naevius), 80
Roof, 91, 92, 93, 105
Rope (Plautus), 84
Rope-walking, 119
Roscius, 112-114, 120, 126
Rupilius, 112

Sabratha, theatre, 104
Sacrifices, 51, 53
Sagalassus, theatre, 99, 100
Salamis, 38, 51, 143
Samnites, 138
Sanctuary of Amphiaros, 45
Sannio, 119, 123
Santra, Pompilius, 82
Sarsina, 83
Saturae, 73
Satyr play, 3, 5, 7, 9, 10, 13-16, 33, 53, 54, 59, 60, 69
Satyrs, 3, 4, 13-15, 60, 65, 79
Scabellum, 120, 122
Scaenae frons, 87, 90, 91, 92, 94, 96, 97, 98, 99, 100, 101, 103, 104, 105, 106, 123
Scaurus, Marcus Aemilius, 87
Scene building, 30, 31, 33, 42-43, 44-45, 87, 93, 96, 97, 101, 103, 104, 105, 106
   See also Skene
Scene painting, 67
Seats, seating, 28, 29, 30, 34, 36, 41, 46, 90, 91, 92, 93, 94, 96-98, 101, 103, 104, 105, 106, 125, 128, 129, 130, 133, 135
Secundus, L. Pomponius, 82
Secutores, 138
Segesta, theatre, 44, 68, 90
Self-Tormentor, The (Terence), 85
Senate, 87, 88, 137
Senators, 125, 141

Seneca, 82, 83
Seven Against Thebes (Aeschylus), 8, 57
Severian map, 96
She-Goat, The, 75
Ship battles: *See* Naumachiae
Shorn Women, The (Menander), 25
Sicilian Expedition, 19
Sicily, Sicilian, 2, 16, 18, 22, 70, 72, 74, 75, 77, 79, 88, 107, 143
Sicyon, 3, 14
   theatre, 44, 46, 68, 100
Sikinnis, 60
Sileni, 4, 15
Silvanus, 73
Silver Age, 117
Siparia, 123
Skene, 30, 31, 32, 34, 36, 37, 39, 42, 43, 45, 46, 67, 68, 99
   See also Scene building
Slaves, 18, 65, 79, 112, 114, 117, 125, 132, 133, 135
Smyrna, 62
Socci, 117, 122
Socrates, 20, 61
Soliloquy, 6, 115
Solon, 6
Song, singing, 1-6, 16, 18, 20, 22, 40, 48, 51, 53, 54, 58, 60, 65, 73, 74, 76, 78, 92, 115, 138
Soothsayers, 9
Sophists, 11, 12, 19, 20
Sophocles, 8, 9-10, 11, 15, 29, 47, 48, 55, 56-57, 59, 67, 68
Sophron, 17
Sorix, 120
Sosias, 21
Sosibius, 18
Sow, The, 85
Spain, 103, 139
Sparta, 18, 19
   theatre, 44
Spartacus, 137
Spectators, 6, 22, 28, 30, 36, 44, 54, 60, 90, 94, 96, 101, 105, 129, 133, 135, 136, 143
   See also Audience
Spina, 129-130, 132, 133

Spinther, 112

Stage scenery and machinery, 31, 54, 67-69, 123-124, 127

Stages, 31, 39, 42, 43, 46, 78, 89, 90, 92, 93, 94, 96, 97, 98, 99, 101, 103, 105, 107, 123, 124

Stairways, 33, 36, 45, 96, 97, 101, 133, 135

Starting gates, 129, 130

Stasimon, 12

Statilius, 112

Statue, 67, 104, 129

Statuette, 22, 24, 64, 74, 81, 118, 122

Steps, 46, 88, 89, 90, 91, 92, 96, 97, 99, 100, 123

Stichus (Plautus), 84

Stilt-walking, 119

Stoa, 33, 34, 67

Stock characters, Middle and New Comedy, 23, 24, 25, 65, 115, 116, 118, 119

Stone theatres, 90, 94-97, 107, 114, 123, 124

Strabo, C. Julius, 82

Stratocles, 114

Stupidus, 119

Suidas, 9, 14, 29

Sulla, 113, 120

Suppliant Maidens, The (Aeschylus), 8, 57

Suppliants, The (Euripides), 10

Susarion, 16, 17

Sword-swallowing, 119

Symmachus, 112

Synchoregoi, 56

Syracuse, 72
    theatre, 30, 44, 68, 124

Syrus, Publilius, 120

Taormina:
    odeum, 93
    theatre, 44, 93

Tarentum, 79

Tarquinius, Prisus Lucius, 128

Tauraus, Statilius, 134

Teacher-director, 57, 65, 67

Telesterion at Eleusis, 93

Temples, 45, 91, 96, 110, 123
    Dionysus, 31, 33, 52
    Flora, 91
    Magna Mater, 91
    Mars Ultor, 142

Temporary wooden theatres, 90-92

Ten Books on Architecture (Vitruvius), 101, 102

Teos, 58

Terence, 41, 83, 84-85, 90, 111, 112, 115, 125

Terentius Lucanus, 84

Termessus, theatre, 99, 100

Tertullian, 96

Thasos, theatre, 44

Theatral areas, Cretan, 28-29

Theatres, 27-28, 41, 43-49, 51-52, 67-70, 90-101, 103-106, 118, 124, 127

Theatron, 27, 30, 31, 33, 36, 37, 41, 43, 44-45, 133

Thebes, 51

Theodora, 120

Theodorus, 59

Theoric fund, 70

Theoritus, 17

Thersilion, 92, 93

Thesmophoriazusae, The (Aristophanes), 20, 68

Thespis, Thespian, 5-7, 12, 16, 56, 60

Thessolus, 59

Thorikos, 51
    theatre, 30, 31

Throne chairs, 34, 41, 70

Thunder, 123-124

Thyestes (Seneca and Varius), 82

Thymele, 29, 33, 36
    See also Altar

Thyromata, 37, 39, 42, 45, 46, 67, 90, 100

Tiber Riber, 72, 143

Tiberius, 114, 128

Timgad, theatre, 104, 124

Titinius, 83

Titus (Emperor), 139

Titus, C. (Roman knight), 82

Tlepolemus, 57

Toga, 117

Trachinian Women, The (Sophocles),
9, 47
Trackers, The (Sophocles), 9, 15
Tragedy:
Greek, 3, 5-12, 13, 14, 15, 16, 18, 23,
29, 31, 33, 40, 46, 47, 48, 54, 55-59,
62-66, 69, 80
Roman, 76, 78, 79-83, 92, 110, 111-117
Tragic recitations, 78, 118
Tragôidia, 6
Tragôidos, 6
Tragos, 6
Tragikoi choroi, 3
Trajan, 139
Tralles, theatre, 68
Tribunalia, 94, 96, 98, 133
Trica, 119
Trident, 138
Trilogy, 8, 9
Trinummus (Plautus), 84
Tripolis, 46
Trireme, 142-143
Tritagōnistēs, 57, 58
Trojan War, 7, 8
Trojan Women, The (Euripides), 10
Trojan Women, The (Seneca), 82
Truculentus (Plautus), 84
Turkey, 27, 41, 44, 46, 70, 93, 99, 103,
104
Turpio, Ambivius, 112
Twin Menaechmi, The (Plautus), 84
Two Baccides (Plautus), 84
Tyndaris, theatre, 44, 90
Tyrants, Greek, 1-3

Tyrian fleet, 141

Underground tunnels, 68, 99, 123

Vaison, theatre, 103, 124
Vallis Murcia, 128
Varius, Rufus, 82
Vase paintings, 13, 14, 15, 17, 88, 89
Vela, velaria, 105, 136
Venationes, 109, 127, 128, 134, 138-140
Venus, 96
Venus Victrix, temple, 96
Verona:
amphitheatre, 133
theatre, 103
Vespasian, 120, 133
Villa of Mysteries at Pompeii, 45
Virgil, 124
Vitruvius, 67, 98, 101-103
Vomitoria, 97

Walkway, sacred, 28
Wasps, The (Aristophanes), 17, 20-22,
57
Wine-Flask, The (Cratinus), 19
Woman of Andros, The (Terence), 85
Women of Trachis, The (Sophocles), 9,
47
Wrestling, 110, 128

Xanthias, 21

Zea, theatre, 44